Animal

Animal

George "the Animal" Steele

with Jim Evans

TRIUMPH
BOOKS

Library of Congress Cataloging-in-Publication Data

Steele, George, 1937–
  Animal / George "the Animal" Steele with Jim Evans.
    pages cm
  ISBN 978-1-60078-798-0
  1. Steele, George, 1937– 2. Wrestlers—United States—Biography. I. Title.
  GV1196.A54A56 2013
  796.812092—dc23
  [B]
                          2013003718

This book is available in quantity at special discounts for your group or organization. For further information, contact:

Triumph Books LLC
814 North Franklin Street
Chicago, Illinois 60610
(312) 337-0747
www.triumphbooks.com

Printed in U.S.A.
ISBN: 978-1-60078-798-0
Design by Patricia Frey
Photos courtesy of the author unless otherwise indicated
Title page photo courtesy of WWE

Contents

Foreword

My friend Jim Myers, aka George "the Animal" Steele, was a ferocious competitor, a standout athlete, and a pro wrestling superstar.

Vince McMahon, the impresario of World Wrestling Entertainment, refers to wrestlers "getting into character" when they perform in the ring or cut a promo on camera, just like Hollywood actors do.

I had a character of my own—Cowboy Bill Watts—during my 25 years in the business, but I did not have to get into character; the character was, and still is, me.

I met Jim before he officially became George "the Animal" Steele, and before I became a professional wrestler. But let me tell you, if you faced him on the football field like I did, you definitely knew he was an animal!

After that explosive and violent first meeting, I wondered about him. Later, after I had entered the pro wrestling world, I saw this character out east named George "the Animal" Steele and wondered if he was the same guy whom I had collided with on the football field that day.

It wasn't until years later, when I was in Philadelphia doing the WWE Hall of Fame induction speech for Ernie Ladd, my dear friend and brother in the Lord, that I saw Jim/George in person again. We reconnected in a much friendlier way and laughed as we recalled how we met. Some time later, after hearing that Jim was fighting a chronic health problem that was on the verge of taking him down for the count, we became even closer.

Jim primarily wrestled during the summer, and then was a teacher and coach during the school year. So, was he two distinct people? No, I think he was just a complex person, multifaceted like a diamond and lovingly polished by his wife, Pat. She has always been there to temper Jim and give him that very special love that we need and are designed to have and need by our Creator to receive. That became even more important in more recent years, thanks to Jim's deep personal relationship with Christ.

To me, the most wonderful aspect of Jim's story is how Christ's love can penetrate even the most hardened, prideful heart. When Jim and I were in the business, God was not a focal point for either of us. Too often, we acted as though were were gods ourselves, whether we admitted it at the time or not. Witnessing Christ reawaken Ernie Ladd's spirit, and Ted DiBiase's, and Jim's—that is the wonder of Christ's love.

I am proud to introduce you to the story of my friend, Jim Myers, aka George "the Animal" Steele, my brother in Christ.

—Cowboy Bill Watts

Introduction

Throughout his entire career as a wrestler, George "the Animal" Steele never spoke a complete sentence. His entire vocabulary was made up of single words: Sky! Pretty! You! Ugly! He ate turnbuckles in the ring. He was hairy. His tongue was green. Fans loved it and wanted more. He was an enigma. Was this guy for real?

To me, George Steele is Jim Myers. I met Jim when I was no more than a boy, in my freshman year of high school. He was my wrestling coach and he scared the hell out of me. He scared the hell out of a lot of people. But he was the best coach a kid could have. My freshman year I didn't win a single match; by senior year, I had made it to the state championships. And Jim was there the whole time, helping me grow up and succeed when I was too young to realize that was what he was doing.

Jim was a life coach before life coaches existed. Without him, I wouldn't have spent 10 years playing professional football. I lost at the state wrestling championships in my senior year. Jim ran out to me on the floor, smacked me across the face, and said, "Kenny, you're going to play college football." At that moment, he snapped me out of my shock at a devastating loss and reminded me that life goes on and that there are other things you can accomplish.

Jim has shown up in my life at the strangest of times. In the 1991 NFC Championship Game, the Detroit Lions played the Washington Redskins. I was on that Lions team and we had never made it that far into the playoffs before. After a dream season, we lost that day, and I sat heartbroken in the locker room with my teammates. At one point I looked up and there was Jim, standing in the doorway. During NFL playoff games, no one gets into the locker room except for the players and the coaches. I don't know how Jim got there, but seeing him made that loss become another lesson to take forward in life.

You're probably wondering if I am talking about the same guy you remember from the ring. I am, and you have to read the book to find out how these two personalities came to be one. You'll be inspired. You'll laugh. Maybe you'll shed a few tears as you read through the pages of this book. When you're done, you too will have a life coach in Jim.

—Kenneth R. Dallafior
Former NFL offensive lineman for the
San Diego Chargers and the Detroit Lions (1985–93)

CHAPTER 1

Who Flunks Second Grade?

My fight with dyslexia began in earnest in grade school. If it had truly been a fight, I would've won. I could have balled up my fists, socked it a few times, and pounded my chest in celebration. Maybe even added a side order of turnbuckle stuffing with gravy. The letters of the alphabet that encircled every classroom would not have appeared to me as though they were hieroglyphics. The abacus that sat near the teacher's desk would have wound up with a black eye, a bloodied nose, and you'd see fewer teeth than in a Crest toothpaste commercial.

But I didn't know anything about dyslexia then. I could not have come close to spelling it on a Scrabble board. Dyslexia is a learning disability few teachers understood back when I was growing up in Madison Heights, a suburb about five miles north of Detroit, Michigan. When I was a kid, measuring intelligence was uncomplicated: you were smart or dumb, bright as a shining star or dim as a 15-watt lightbulb. Our grade school class was divided into different reading groups: bluebirds, redbirds, yellow birds, and brown birds. I roosted among the brown birds, which meant I could not read worth a crap.

We read aloud about fun with a couple of kids named Dick and Jane. Well, there was nothing fun about stammering. I don't care if Dick was sledding and Jane was skating or they both were playing with a dog named Spot. I did not know anyone named Dick, did not care about anyone named Jane, and thought Spot was a mighty simplistic name for a mutt.

But Dick and Jane were the main characters in reading books written by William S. Gray and Zerna Sharp. They were used in pretty much every school this side of the School of Rock to teach kids to read from the 1930s to the 1970s. The focus was to develop the Curriculum Foundation Series of books for Scott Foresman and Company.

Dick, Jane, Spot, Baby, Mother, Father, Puff the cat, and Tim the teddy bear ganged up to become the banes of my existence. Oh, see. Oh, see Jane. Funny, funny Jane. It was not the least bit funny to me. Oh, see. Oh, see Jim. Unfunny, unfunny Jim Myers.

The drawings were simplistic and so were the words, but not to me. The text was all in black and white, but nothing about reading was black and white to me. Everything fell into the gray area.

Honestly, I would have loved to have told my story and never mentioned these struggles in school. That is a chunk of my life I do not enjoy recalling. Even all these years later, the embarrassment still stings. I would have loved to have been the kid who won the spelling bee, the one who got the shiny red apple from the teacher and not vice versa. I would have been proud to have been a National Honor Society member, one of those kids who gives speeches on high school graduation day. But that would have been dishonest. Dyslexia is a part of me, and if writing about it helps someone, then it is worthwhile. If your children are having problems in school, get them help. Do not write them off as being dumb as a cinder block. Don't call them stupid as a Kardashian.

Just call the school principal. Call the school psychologist. Get them some help.

Unfortunately, I was just written off as dumb. My report card was filled with *E*s and *F*s, two letters I had no trouble deciphering. That is the way it was back then.

Consequently, I hated school and despised the laughter and taunts of my classmates. I tried to disappear, which is not easy unless your name is Copperfield or D.B. Cooper. Since I was the biggest kid in class, it was especially difficult. It would have been like King Kong trying to blend in with the jockeys at Churchill Downs. When I was called on by the teacher, I hated school even more. I'd get up in front of the class and it was as though I had a mouth full of malted milk balls. I stuttered and stammered and the other kids in school would start laughing.

That is why I especially hated the desk my parents bought when I was in the first grade. That's where I sat for hours after school trying in vain to learn my lessons while my classmates played in the schoolyard across the street. That desk became a symbol of all my frustrations. It was big and wooden and as foreboding as an angry teacher's stare.

Still, it was important to both my mom and dad that I got a good education, and that is why Dad put a bear hug on the anemic family budget to buy that desk. It was where I was to study and do my homework. It was a gift from my parents. But it was also a curse.

After school, I would spend hours at that desk. I could not go outside to play until I studied my vocabulary words. I also had to do my arithmetic and my reading. That was like locking a person in solitary confinement and telling them to enjoy the conversation. The harder I tried, the more difficult it got. My dad was a very patient man, but he became very frustrated trying to help me learn. Dad never realized that what he was seeing on those pages was not what I was seeing at all.

Dad never had the opportunity to get a good education himself. The youngest of 13 children, he came to Michigan with his mother. By then, all of his brothers and sisters had already left home. His father had died.

My dad's family was almost literally blown out of Oklahoma by the Dust Bowl of the 1930s that lasted nearly a decade. The wrath was felt by a lot more folks than the Joads, the characters in *The Grapes of Wrath*. "Car-loads, caravans, homeless and hungry; twenty thousand and fifty thousand and a hundred thousand and two hundred thousand. They streamed over the mountains, hungry and restless—restless as ants, scurrying to find work to do—to lift, to push, to pull, to pick, to cut—anything, any burden to bear, for food. The kids are hungry. We got no place to live. Like ants scurrying for work, for food, and most of all for land."

Grasslands had been deeply plowed into oblivion. Wheat was planted, and when Mother Nature kicked in with her PMS tears, the rainfall produced bountiful crops. But as the droughts of the early 1930s descended, no matter how much plowing the farmers did, nothing would grow. Crops withered and died, and so did dreams of living off the land. Winds whipped across the plains and even daytime turned dark.

When Franklin D. Roosevelt took office as president in March 1933, the country was in bad shape. FDR quickly shored up the banking industry, and also enacted the Emergency Farm Mortgage Act and the Farm Credit Act.

In 1937, Roosevelt's second inaugural address prefaced those of Steinbeck in *The Grapes of Wrath*: "I see one-third of the nation ill-housed, ill-clad, ill-nourished...the test of our progress is not whether we add more to the abundance of those who have much; it is whether we provide enough for those who have too little." FDR's Shelterbelt Project began. The project called for large-scale planting of trees across the Great Plains to protect the land from erosion, stretching in a 100-mile-wide zone from Canada to northern Texas. Native trees, such as red cedar and green ash, were planted along fencerows separating properties, and farmers were paid to plant and cultivate them. The project was estimated to cost $75 million and would be done over a period of 12 years.

In the fall of 1939, the rains finally came. Dad, just 15, had already gone to work at Briggs Manufacturing. He realized how important his lack of education was. His résumé, if he even had one, was long on sweat and grime and short on pay scale. An extremely hard worker, he was never what you would call a white-collar employee. His shirts were neither white nor starched nor remotely unsullied. He was part of the rank and file, and while that never bothered Dad, he was determined to provide his son with more opportunities.

To him, that meant a great education. Times were very tough, but Dad made sure we had encyclopedias in the house. They did not all arrive at once, but soon enough we had the entire set. He made sure there were word books. There were children's classics. "Puss in Boots" was more important than new shoes. Mother Hubbard wasn't the only one with bare cupboards, but Dad did the best he could. We had a dictionary and I had the desk.

I was actually very excited about starting school. Before I was in kindergarten, my mother used to take me across the street to recite rhymes to the older kids. I was just three years old when that started. I did great, too. I could out-honk Mother Goose when it came to those nursery rhymes.

But it really hit the fan when I started school. Reading and math were the toughest. I could not spell, so I would write so sloppily the teacher could not tell I had misspelled so many words. I had a hard time deciphering even the simplest words.

I even failed the second grade. Who, this side of a character in an Adam Sandler comedy, flunks second grade? That same year, I remember a visiting teacher taking me to a place in Detroit to be tested. I did the

Rorschach Test with the inkblots. Everything to me looked like a Bic pen had exploded onto two sheets of paper. I strung together beads by color and analyzed pictures. I remember they showed me one picture of the wind blowing the trees one way, while some clothes hung on a line were blowing the other way, and then asked me what was wrong with the picture. Now, I may have been dyslexic, but I was not dumb. It was pretty obvious what was wrong. Afterward, I heard them talking about me in the other room. They said I had tested well and was even bright in many ways.

It was very important to my father that he owned a home. Dad took out a $100 loan and bought a small lot. He built the home himself, using lumber because it was cheaper. My dad was a very hardworking person, but he did not have cotton candy hair and his name was not Trump. The words *disposable* and *income* never met in our house. We barely had enough to get by. Dad did the plumbing and electrical himself, too.

Three years later, we moved out of our house. Times were tough, and housing was at a premium as World War II began. My folks opted to rent out our home and moved us into the garage. It was not as bad as that sounds. Dad had built the garage out of cement blocks; it had a toilet and sinks, so it was really better than most houses in the neighborhood. Many of the other folks still had outhouses. I get tears in my eyes when I look at the many pictures that my parents took of me between the ages of two and four. By 1943, we moved back into our home.

I was seven when my brother, Jack, was born. Jack would go on to become superintendent of the Madison (Michigan) Schools. I was also seven when I flunked the second grade. I was a total wreck. Everybody else in class wore bright smiles, freckles, and pigtails. I specialized in a turtlenecked glower. I was just a big, lumbering dummy. I was the only one wearing XL clothes in a sea of children's sizes. I was also the only one who flunked. I mean, that is ridiculous. A man named Donald Gardner once wrote, "All I want for Christmas is my two front teeth, my two front teeth, see my two front teeth…"

Well, I wanted some understanding, too.

With apologies to the Audubon Society, something I have a little trouble understanding even now is why I traded my yo-yo to someone in the neighborhood for his alleged talking crow. I was 11 and the talking crow was his sales pitch. Little did I know that the crow was really sick. Any sicker and Jack Kevorkian would have been perched on a branch outside our house croaking "Nevermore!" On just the second day that I owned it and not my yo-yo, the crow fell off my shoulder. An attorney might have referred to his demise as *ex crow facto*. I was crushed. Obviously the bird did not come with a yo-yo-back guarantee.

Jack and I had a time-honored ritual back then: we would take any animals that had died to the backyard, dig a hole, and bury them. We even said a prayer or two. So when the crow croaked and did not caw, we went to the backyard, dug a hole about 18 inches deep, and began to officially lay the crow to rest. We put the defunct bird in the hole, threw some dirt on it, and all of a sudden, the crow went "Brrrrr!"

Was it a resurrection of Biblical proportions, or did we prematurely bury the bird? Jack and I frantically got down on our knees, yanked the bird from its grave, apologetically brushed it off, and pronounced it alive. At least Jack did. I still was not too sure. It was still the deadest-looking living bird I had ever seen. Its wings were hanging at half mast; its head was hanging like one of Judge Roy Bean's customers; and if it was breathing at all, its breath was shallower than that grave.

After a few minutes, we once again declared it dead, put it back into the ground, threw dirt on it, and again it went "Brrrrr!"

That is the script we followed at least twice more. Dead or alive? It was a wanted poster in black feathers. Finally, I'd had enough. I was going to kill that damnable bird myself. I took the shovel and smacked it. I smacked it again and again. Then I chopped at it. I was a hibachi chef in a chicken coop. I was enraged. I wanted my yo-yo back. I wanted this crow gone.

Later on, Jack and I realized what had happened. The crow had been dead the entire time, but every time we threw dirt on its carcass, some air was forced out of its lungs.

That sound still gives me shivers to this day. So does the recollection of reading with the brown birds. School was definitely crappy.

CHAPTER 2
The Fight Game

Despite having dispatched the crow, I'd always been taught not to fight. Turn the other cheek, even if you had just been socked in that same place. An eye for an eye? Well, even if that eye had turned black and blue thanks to a punch, that was not the Golden Rule as practiced at the Myers house in Madison Heights.

Early on, the Animal was caged.

My parents were worried that if I ever fought I would hurt someone. Remember, I was bigger than my classmates. I was Jethro Bodine and my classmates were Opie Taylor. If a fight did break out, and some little punk with spaghetti for arms and a pretzel rod for a neck smacked me, I would run home crying. Those were mostly tears of embarrassment and anger, but it did not matter. I quickly gained a reputation as a big wimp.

I'd been playing ball with some of the guys on the playground at Koss (Schoenhals) Elementary School. It was one of those hot summer days when the camels are applying Hawaiian Tropic and Bedouins are at Sears buying air conditioners.

Animal

I was called home. The guys asked me to bring them back some cold water. Well, I found out that we were going visiting and my mom had me dress in my best clothes. I took a pail of icewater back to the playground so the guys could have a drink before we left. After they finished their drinks, they took what was left and poured it on me. I ran home crying, as usual.

That was it. My mother had finally had it. She exploded like Mt. Vesuvius in Aqua Net hairspray. She told me that it was time for me to stick up for myself. I started crying even harder. She got this big piece of wood and brandished it menacingly. She asked if she would have to beat me before I fought. I was sobbing and sniffling as my mom marched me across the street to the playground. She announced that her Jimmy was there to fight. The kids, who were still laughing, began to laugh even harder. That only irritated my mom more. She asked them who wanted to be first. They all ran to accept the challenge, and Mickey Folton won the race. Mickey was one tough hombre, but it only took me about 30 seconds to kick his butt. Not only did I kick it, I turned it into steak tartare. Two more kids accepted the challenge, and two more raced home looking for Band-Aids and solace. Three up and three down, and the rest of the kids scattered.

Success comes in many different forms. The businessman and his Brooks Brothers suits and Porsche. The actress with her name on the top of the marquee. The baseball player who has just hit a home run that traveled so far its flight plan had to be filed with the FAA. Well, those fights in the playground were my first real successes, and from that day on I embraced fighting. I took to it like Charlie Sheen to tiger blood. It was the one thing I was good at. Success is an excellent motivator, and I had suddenly become a successful fighter.

I know that sounds like a lousy life plan. Real ambition in school should have a book bag attached to it. It should be written in pencil lead and topped with an *A* scrawled by a teacher. But I am going to

20

be redundant here. School was nothing but frustration for me. Try as I might, I could never get things right. Reading was nearly an impossibility and math might as well have been quantum physics wrapped in Latin and served on a kaiser roll. Some kids relished it when the teacher handed back their papers. Those were the kids who always wore smiles to class. Unlike them, my dress code included scowls.

Until I punched somebody out. That was my way of getting an A. That was my National Honor Society membership, and my chance to leapfrog to the front of the class. Satisfaction comes in many different packages, and a clenched fist and a bloodied nose was the way mine was wrapped.

The Animal was uncaged.

I guess that shows you the depth of my frustration as I tried in vain to deal with dyslexia. That wasn't really Mickey Folton I was beating the bejabbers out of. It was every failed math test, every garbled chapter of reading. It was an exorcism of sorts, minus Linda Blair's rotating head and vomit the shade of split-pea soup.

I kept flunking classes and winning fights. I was a total misfit in the classroom and a bully in the halls. Consequently, I did not run with the regular high school kids. If you carried a math book and wore a pocket protector, then I was nowhere to be seen in your zip code. I hung out with an older crowd. I ran with losers and dropouts. Class presidents did not ride shotgun with us. No one in the school played around in our group.

As a ninth grader, I had my first fight in high school. I put a pretty good whipping on a senior, Henry Parker. I don't even remember what the fight was all about. Henry was actually a really good guy. But that fight gave me instant reputation as a tough guy at Madison High School. When it came to homecoming kings, I had my own way of crowning them.

Animal

I was in quite a few fights, and most of the time they were with guys who were older than me. One of many that really stood out occurred when I was just 15 years old. My buddy, Dave Pierce, stopped by my house and asked me to go for a ride. When we got to the car, Dave told me he had a problem with a big guy. It should've been plural. There were actually two guys, and he thought the smaller guy might have a gun. Dave was going to fight the big guy and he wanted to make sure the little guy stayed on the sideline and did not get involved.

We met these two jerks behind Romaine's Drugstore in nearby Royal Oak. The big guy looked like he'd been drinking steroid cocktails every day for the last five years. His biceps were the size of beach balls. His neck was carved from a sequoia. The little guy was all sorts of greasy, like Ratso Rizzo in *Midnight Cowboy*. My buddy Dave was about 5'10" and 170 pounds. I knew what was coming. Dave took his best shot, which for him was to kick the guy so hard in the family jewels that he instantly became a gelding. When the big guy went down, Dave got on top and straddled him, throwing as many punches as possible. It was like David was once again besting Goliath. Only this particular Goliath was not giving up easily. He reached up and got Dave by the head and began to pound it on the concrete parking lot. Blood started to flow. I thought Dave was going to get killed. I was standing to the right of the little guy, which was perfect because I'm a lefty. I decked him and at the same time I did a Lou Groza number on the big guy's face. I kicked him so hard that I am sure his cheek was tattooed with the word *Florsheim*. I was sure I heard something break, and the big guy rolled over and started shaking like he was having a fit. I thought I had killed him.

The next day at school, the rumors were flying. The big guy had just gotten out of Jackson Prison, he was a heavyweight boxing champion, he was a power lifting champion, he ate small children for lunch and their dads for dinner. His name was Paul Bunyan; he had an ox named Babe and an ox to gore by the name of Jim Myers. Supposedly he was going to come to Madison High to kill me. Well, two nights later the same guy was caught with another man's wife and got shot in the face. In the process, he hurt someone really badly and was sent back to jail. What a relief! But for a long time I heard stories that the big guy had sworn to get me.

Dave was my best friend throughout high school, even though he did not stay around for much school. His dad owned a landscaping company and convinced him that laying sod and planting trees was preferable to reading, writing, and 'rithmetic. As soon as Dave could legally drop out, he did. He was 16 years old.

In the language of professional wrestling, Dave could have been called a tag team partner. We always head each other's backs. Once Dave picked me up in a sweet 1953 Oldsmobile. He had just bought it used and it was around Christmastime. We took it into Royal Oak, and right when we started to cross some railroad tracks, it stalled. A split second later, the lights started flashing and the railroad crossing gates came down. A train was coming! We kept looking at each other; is that train going to hit us or not? We were not quite straddling the tracks, but that big Olds was definitely in harm's way. Nothing a frantic Dave could do would coax that car to turn over. We finally jumped out of the car, and a couple of seconds later, the car was on the losing end of a huge collision with a racing train. Dave did not have any insurance on the vehicle either.

At that time in my life, God was about the furthest thing from my mind. I was just a kid; what did I know about divine presence? The Bible was just another book I had trouble reading. All I knew was that after the car had been hit, it had careened past me and slammed into the same signal post I was trying to sprint to hide behind it. Believe me, after that close call, I thanked a lot of things—four-leaf clovers, horseshoes, dumb luck, and good fortune—but not God. God and I hadn't been introduced yet. I wouldn't have known Him if He had been sitting next to me on the sideline during a football game. Those formal introductions would not come until many, many years later. But I had to wonder how come that car hadn't turned me into Maypo? Somebody was looking out for me besides just my harried mom and dad.

Fights were not my only outlet in school. I had picked up the nickname "Moose," and sports gave me an outlet that I also embraced. Football, after all, was just a legalized street fight. I could smack guys around and get the congratulations of my teammates instead of phone calls from the principal or the police. It was perfect for me. The harder I hit our opponents, the more the coaches and my teammates liked it.

There was no three-second rule in basketball in those days. I could have set up a pup tent and lit a Coleman stove in the lane and the refs would not have cared. Essentially, that is what I would do. I would plant myself under the backboard and take ownership of that chunk of real estate. If it truly was a non-contact sport the way Doc Naismith had imagined, I took liberties with the rules. Pushing and shoving were part of the job description. If I was not using my elbows, then I was not playing.

Somehow, I was even able to turn baseball into a contact sport. I played first base. I cannot count the number of runners who fell down rounding first against me. I also was on the track and field team, but that did not offer a lot as far as physical contact goes. I tossed the shot, and that was about it.

CHAPTER 3

Speaking in Tongues

I first joined a football team in junior high in 1951 and immediately became one of its stars. That is probably no surprise. Size does matter, especially in most sports. I was among the biggest players on the field, and definitely the most ornery.

Madison High School had hired a new football coach, Don Scott. Coach Scott also taught seventh-grade history and he told me that I was going out for all the junior high sports. I certainly was not going to argue. That is where I had the best chance for success.

I can't tell you how excited I was when I got my first football uniform and pads. I went right home and put my uniform on my brother, Jack. I placed two rocks about five feet apart. I was on my knees and I made Jack run between the rocks to work on my tackling skills. At the time, I was much bigger than he was. He literally became my tackling dummy. Jack went on to become a small college All-American at Western State University in Gunnison, Colorado, and was drafted by George "Papa

Bear" Halas and the Chicago Bears. But that was years later. As a little kid, he was on the wrong end of "Brother Dearest."

One day during a game I went to tackle a much smaller kid. It was like the shark from *Jaws* getting ready to munch on Disney's Nemo. I had a habit of sticking my tongue out when I strained from physical effort. That was long before Michael Jordan stole my act and turned it into his trademark. All of a sudden, this little guy's helmet came up and smacked me in the chin. There was no such thing as facemasks in those days and chin guards offered about as much protection as Saran Wrap.

I almost bit my tongue in half. Blood was spurting out, and pretty soon it looked as if I had guzzled a whole pitcher of strawberry Kool-Aid.

Back then, the doctor really did not know what to do with an injury like that, so he put a small disc in my tongue, sewed it up, and sent me home. Have you ever tried to talk with a tongue that has turned black and was so swollen it barely fit in your mouth? Enunciation, never my strong point, started wandering way off the beaten track. Finding the right sounds was akin to herding cats with a whisk broom. I knew what I was saying, but nobody else did.

Talking was not the only trouble I had, either. Swallowing became a big problem, too.

I was like that for six months.

That made for an unpleasant introduction to a new teacher who came into the classroom for the second semester. Our regular teacher was on maternity leave. The new teacher introduced herself and then had each class member stand up and tell her what we had done for Christmas. It was her way of getting to know us.

Let me remind you that my tongue was still as black as a piece of coal. While I was never exactly a Dale Carnegie grad anyway, I could not get words out at all. I sat in the back of the room in an attempt to hide, but when you are 6'0" and weigh 220 pounds in the seventh grade, hiding is not really an option. My facial stubble did not help, either.

When it was my turn to stand up and speak, I was already sweating. Even though my 5 Day Deodorant Pad was only on its second shift, it did not matter. I said, "Mh naam is Gemm Marrs." The teacher looked at me with disdain. Her reply; "Sit down, dummy. You cannot even talk."

An oddly colored tongue. An inability to speak intelligently. A crudely constructed audition for my later life as George "the Animal" Steele? Heaven knows what the blueprint was, but it can be awfully strange the way things work out. This was years before I ever considered carrying a foreign object in my trunks or eating the stuffing out of wrestling ring turnbuckles. Nobody was concerned about a high-fiber diet when I was a seventh grader.

Way back then, I sported hair on my head and not on my back.

While I can chuckle about it now, my inability to articulate was a humiliating incident when it occurred. Humiliated, I did not talk in a classroom again until I was a sophomore in college.

Somebody call Linda Blair. It was just more frustration that needed to be exorcised by athletics.

I will never forget my first day of high school football. I was a freshman. Rod Hogan was a junior. He had red hair the color of Bozo the Clown. He was about 6'3" and weighed 230 pounds. Unlike yours truly, Rod was never short on words. He was a big talker and had convinced me that he was tougher than beef jerky.

Coach Scott had us form two lines for a tackling drill. The coach pitched the ball to me and Rod was about 10 yards away. He was making this wild sound, and if looks could kill, a bugle would have been blowing "Taps" at the 50-yard line. Rod ran at me and I ran full tilt at him. I knew the ensuing collision would register about 7.2 on the Richter scale, and I was ready for the hit. I put my head down and leaned forward to get ready. I wound up falling on my face because tough Rod Hogan had turned Colonel Sanders at the last second. He had chickened out and stepped aside to avoid contact. When I realized what had just happened, I figured I was really something special. I was feeling pretty darn good about myself and nearly sprinted back to line to await my next victim.

Across the way loomed Babe Erikson, a senior. Well, it was déjà boo hoo.

Coach Scott pitched me the ball and this time I was full of confidence. I pranced toward Babe like a freshly groomed poodle full of talc. My head was up and my eyes were wide open. Babe Erikson not only tackled me, he drove me backward about eight yards, and the first thing that hit the ground was the back of my helmet. I hit the ground so hard I thought I heard Rod Serling doing his intro to *The Twilight Zone*. Thank God for that helmet. If I hadn't been wearing some sort of protection on my head, I would have been combing a patch of rye grass instead of hair. As I slowly got up, Babe leaned over and said "Welcome to football, kid."

What great timing and what a great lesson to learn. I never forgot it. Respect all and fear none.

I loved sports and I hated class. That was an inexorable equation. But I did not have squatter's rights on frustration. The teachers in high school were themselves getting frustrated with my inability to grasp their lessons. They did not send me to the office. Instead, my return address at Madison High was frequently the gym or shop class.

The teachers simply did not know what to do with me. I was still having a difficult time dealing with dyslexia. The written word might as well have been Sanskrit. Or maybe Klingon. Reading was an exercise in despair wrapped in frustration. Spelling was akin to figuring out the Theory of Relativity, and I certainly was not Einstein.

According to the National Center of Learning Disabilities, children and adults with dyslexia have a neurological disorder that causes their brains to process and interpret information differently. It is not a sign of poor intelligence or laziness. It is not the result of impaired vision. Dyslexia is a lifelong challenge that sufferers are born with.

Dyslexia occurs among people of all economic and ethnic backgrounds. As many as 15 percent of Americans have major troubles with reading.

Much of what happens in a classroom is based on reading and writing. So it's important to identify dyslexia as early as possible. Using alternate learning methods, people with dyslexia can achieve success.

The trouble was, when I was in school, little was understood about dyslexia or other learning disabilities. To reiterate, you were either smart or stupid. Or, in this case, you were either in algebra class or in gym class; in the biology lab or in wood shop.

More often than not, the teachers would take attendance and then send me to either shop class or the gym. Those became my classrooms of choice.

The only thing I was successful at in school was the physical stuff. That meant sports and fighting. When I was not in class, Don Scott made me a hall monitor. Naturally, I changed into a hall *monster*.

I was a Brinks security guard with an attitude. I was George "the Animal" Steele with khakis and a button-down shirt. The halls were mine. They were my domain. I knew who should be walking through them and who should not. Nobody was allowed in my halls without a pass. That was unacceptable.

Something else that was unacceptable occurred when a bunch of kids from Pershing High School in Detroit came to my school looking to cause trouble for some of our seniors. There had been a fight between them the previous weekend.

Animal

Don Scott took me out to the parking lot with him when these kids from Detroit showed up. I was only a freshman or maybe a sophomore, but I was as at least as big as anyone else, and I certainly was not scared. Did you ever see the movie *The Ghost and Mr. Chicken*? Well, in class I was Don Knotts, but in the parking lot or on the athletic field, I was certainly Not Don. I had a different personality, and it was generally an aggressive one. While we were out in the parking lot and Coach Scott was telling the kids from Pershing to go home, I tried to show how tough I was by spitting between my teeth. Of course, the spittle went all over one of the Pershing guy's shoes. They wound up leaving anyway and a rumble was avoided.

Coach Scott was also the truant officer. He was all about discipline. Once when a kid skipped school, the coach walked right into his house and dragged him out and back to class. You could not get away with that these days. Every attorney this side of the late F. Lee Bailey would be lining up at the door waiting to sue Don Scott, the Madison School District, and probably the manufacturer of the lock on the door of the kid's home.

Coach Scott always looked out for me, and for that I am forever grateful.

Somebody else who always looked out of me (as well as all of the other kids in Madison Heights) was my late mom, Lois, who wound up spending 29 years on the Madison school board. Unlike her oldest son, she had been a great student. More like me, she had also been a great athlete. In high school, she played basketball and softball. She was so good that the boys would let her practice with them. Her family came to Michigan from Georgia. They took the bus north to Detroit and were told to get off at the Grand River stop. They all kept looking for a river, but Grand River in the Motor City is an avenue lined with residences and commercial buildings. The only water running there came from faucets and garden hoses.

Mom coached a Class C baseball team when I was younger. There was nobody else to manage the team, so my mom did it. I was the bat boy and was exposed to both sports and being around older boys.

Mom truthfully was a very special person—not just to her own family, but to a lot of other people. Even before I started grade school, she was running a teen club for the high school kids. She touched the lives of a lot of folks through the programs she started. Everything she did was aimed at helping kids and providing them with opportunities.

Our high school gym was very small. There were maybe two rows of chairs around the sides of the basketball court, and some bleachers at one end where the stage happened to be. A foam mat hung from the wall at the other end so that anyone going in for a layup or trying to save a ball from going out of bounds would not maim himself.

We were playing Keego Harbor High School one night and a kid sitting on the stage decided to turn off the lights while play was still going on. The gym went dark just as a Keego Harbor player went in for a layup.

When the lights came back on, that player was sprawled out on the court. His name was O'Shaugnessy and he was their star player. Honest to Thomas Edison, I did not do anything to him when the lights were out. I swear on a stack of polygraph exams I did not hit him. I don't think anybody on my team did. Instead, I think he smacked into the wall because he suddenly could not see a thing. But because of my reputation and penchant for rough play, I was definitely the prime suspect in the minds of the Keego Harbor fans. I was a rough player who protected the lane as if it had been deeded to me. People streamed out of the stands and onto the court. There was pushing and shoving and maybe a couple of punches thrown. It was not pretty, and nobody was particularly proud of the way things ended.

Unfortunately, as the schedule dictated, we played in Keego Harbor a couple of weeks later. Tensions were definitely high, and when our bus pulled into the school parking lot, a couple of police cars immediately flanked it. Five of six police officers walked us into the building, and two of them were my personal escorts. They walked us to the locker room and told us to stay put until right before the game was to begin.

There was a running track above the court, and that was where most of the Keego Harbor students were. They used rubber bands to shoot bobby pins at us throughout the entire game. I remember going to the free throw line and getting stung on the back of the neck once or twice.

Other than the bobby pins, I don't remember any other incidents. The police marched us back to the bus and gave us an escort out of town.

My mom; my brother, Jack; and my girlfriend, Pat were at that game. When the Keego Harbor fans spotted them and realized that they were my family, they started to shake the car. Pat and my mom were petrified, but Jack took charge and they drove out of there as quickly as they could.

Pat was undoubtedly the best thing to happen to me in high school, regardless of how many fights or games I won. Do you know about *Beauty and the Beast*? Well, put a little more body hair on the Beast and that pretty much sums us up as a couple.

It all started with a dare. I had never dated anyone, but a Sadie Hawkins dance was coming up and one of Pat's girlfriends posed a laughable question: "Who is going to ask Moose Myers?" It was delivered as a punch line more than a serious question, and it was only by divine grace that Pat decided that she would ask me to the dance.

She was everything I was not in school. She was beautiful, got good grades, and was active in everything that good kids were involved in, including cheerleading, yearbook, and the National Honor Society. Me, I could barely read the yearbook, and I was about as qualified for the

National Honor Society as I was for the Mensa Society, which is to say, not at all.

I did not dance, and Pat loved to dance, but we went to the Sadie Hawkins Dance anyway. For some unfathomable reason, Pat decided we should keep dating after that night.

More than a half-century later, we are still going out. I thank God every day for Pat taking that dare. I thanked God every day, even before I knew who God was.

CHAPTER 4

A Spartan Existence

Was I college material? Considering my problems in school, there were those who had serious doubts. My test scores were so low you needed a pick and shovel to find them. My grade-point average was not exactly the stuff of the Ivy League. The Poison Ivy League, maybe—complete with the itching, scratching, and generally uncomfortable feeling I had when standing in front of a class.

But I could play football, and the idea of a student-athlete was loosely applied in certain cases. I was not going to college with an eye toward medical school. I was going to school with an eye on creating medical conditions on the football field. My major would be mayhem and my minor would be havoc.

So, which institution of higher learning would I lower the standards of? For the longest time, the University of Notre Dame was the front runner. They had an excellent football program, and with Touchdown Jesus residing near the stadium, I figured a little divine inspiration might go a long way. But no women were allowed on the campus in South Bend, and since Pat and I had already gotten married, that was a rule we definitely could not abide by. Our daughter, Felicia, was a little young to be joining a sorority or even don a cheerleader's outfit.

Luckily, there were other options and doesn't that seem incredible based on my academic trials and tribulations in high school? You needed the Hubble Telescope to spot my academic potential, thanks to my dyslexia.

I ended up at Michigan State University, where I would star on head coach Duffy Daugherty's outstanding football teams.

When word got out that I had chosen Michigan State, there was a bit of a media buzz. The *Detroit Times* ran a story on the sports page, complete with a picture of Pat and me holding Felicia. I was asked where we were going to live in East Lansing, and I said that we would be the first ones to move into the new Spartan Village apartments when the complex opened. Duffy had not told me that this was supposed to be a secret, and when the story came out, all hell broke loose on campus. There was already a long waiting list of married students already waiting for Spartan Village to open. A lot of them had been living in Quonset huts, those half-moon-shaped metal structures with "plush" accommodations that did not always include indoor plumbing. Every time it rained, you would have sworn Buddy Rich was on the roof doing a drum solo. I had already caused the head of housing some major problems and I had not even arrived on campus yet.

As things turned out, that furor was just a preview of my college career.

I graduated from Madison High in January. I started my education at MSU in the spring of 1956 and lived in the Kellogg Center, which was the training facility for the hotel and restaurant management students.

Pat and Felicia stayed home and lived with her parents that semester. At the Kellogg Center, I enjoyed the best living quarters on campus. I ate great food and signed for my meals. I had fresh linens regularly. I had everything but a nightly mint on my pillow.

I was also able to take part in spring football with the varsity team and found out quickly I was able to hold my own. At the end of spring ball, Duffy called me in and congratulated me on a fine spring. The trouble was, he was not sure what to do with me. Freshmen were not allowed to play varsity football back then. I was given a choice of working out in the fall with the varsity or the incoming freshmen. I made a poor decision by choosing to join the incoming freshmen. In hindsight, I needed the challenge and discipline that went along with the varsity program.

The first day the incoming freshmen met in the Spartan Stadium locker room I met John Baum. He was a big tackle who announced in a very loud voice that he could pin anyone in the locker room. I immediately jumped at the challenge. I asked him what made him believe he could pin me. He replied that he was a two-time state wrestling champion. I told him that did not impress me, and that there was no way he could pin me.

The problem with my proclamation was that I did not know the first thing about wrestling. So, with the entire MSU freshman football team gathered in the middle of the field, John Baum proceeded to turn me into an extra-large pretzel, minus the salt. I was as strong as he was, but he used my strength against me. What an embarrassing experience. I knew then that I needed to learn how to wrestle.

He was also married and had a family. John and his wife, Nancy, became our closest friends over the next five years.

Pat and Felicia joined me after my first semester. I said good-bye to the Kellogg Center and hello to a very small apartment in Williamston, a small town about 15 miles from campus. Pay phone booths and gas station bathrooms were spacious by comparison. I said good-bye to the plush life of a future football star, too. I hitchhiked to and from campus.

Animal

We were beyond broke. We could not even afford the felt-tip pen it would've taken to scrawl a sign that read WILL WORK FOR FOOD. Pat's parents would come visit us one weekend, and my parents would come the next weekend. They brought us food and other things we needed.

I remember one Friday when we were out of almost everything. Old Mother Hubbard and her bare cupboards did not have anything over us. It was one of those gray Michigan days in March when the sky looks like it is wearing a banker's gray flannel suit. The only things we had to eat were a jar of Gerber's mushed carrots for Felicia, and one strip of bacon in an otherwise deserted Frigidaire. I went out for a walk in the backyard and wandered over to where a garden had been the previous spring and summer. I could not believe what I saw: a cabbage that had somehow survived the long, cold winter. I felt as if I had stubbed my toe on a porterhouse steak with all the trimmings. I ripped that cabbage out of the frozen ground and raced upstairs to show Pat. She proceeded to boil the cabbage and added the strip of bacon for a little flavor. We all had dinner together, Felicia eating her carrots while Pat and I split the cabbage. Pat had a little dog named Cotton, and Cotton got the bacon. I looked on enviously at Cotton. If we had been any hungrier, we would have been eating a hot dog dinner...literally. Needless to say, when Pat's mom and dad came to visit the next day with their typical care package, Cotton accompanied them on the return trip home. Since we could not even afford Alpha-Bits, we could hardly spend any money on Alpo. Where was the privileged life of a big-time college athlete?

There was a gravel pit behind the apartment in Williamston. I would work out there and would regularly see this guy on the other side of the pond. He would run sprints and swim lengths across the pond. We would always wave to one another and keep on working out. When we met a few years later, we remembered each other. The man was Ed Farhat, the original Iron Sheik and one of the wildest men in the history of the wrestling business.

Wild is not the way I would characterize Reserve Officers' Training Corps (ROTC). I was totally unprepared for that experience. Because Michigan State was a land-grant university, every male student back then was required to take part in ROTC for two years. I hated it, but I had no choice. I had to join, and I picked the air force over the army program.

We took military classes, which was fine with me. But in the spring and fall we had to dress in full uniform and march the parade field. I was extremely self-conscious and did not like playing like a soldier. I felt like a counterfeit G.I. Joe.

On this particular day, rain had turned the turf on the parade field into mud. A young officer got in my face. We were nose to nose. He told me I had some mud on my shoes and ordered me to take a handkerchief and wipe them off. I exploded and punched this guy right between the eyes. He flew back about three feet and landed on his rear end. I told him to take his handkerchief out and wipe the mud off his butt. That bit of stupidity got me an F for a grade in R.O.T.C. It also made me ineligible to play football my sophomore year.

It was hardly the first time I acted like a real turkey while at MSU, and it would not be the last.

The football office got me a job with Grainger Brothers Construction in the summer of 1958. I worked really hard and the foreman took a liking to me. The Grainger brothers had projects going all over the campus, so every school break I had a job waiting for me. Believe me, we needed the money.

During one Christmas break, I drove Pat and Felicia back home so they could spend some time with our parents. Then I went back to campus to work. It was really frigid that winter. I was a laborer for the bricklayers—my job was to keep them stocked with bricks and mud. On Friday, it got so cold we had to stop work because the mud was freezing. We were all huddled in a shanty waiting for our checks when this wild game of In Between (aces being high and deuces being low) broke out.

The rules were simple: the dealer would give you two cards up, and you could bet any amount or fold. If you chose to stay in and the next card was in between your first two cards, you won and took out of the pot whatever you bet. If you lost, you put whatever you bet in the pot.

I was playing just to kill time. I would bet a dollar when it seemed like I had a chance to win. I got an ace and a deuce and covered the pot. I got another ace. The pot was about $300, my check for the week was going to be about $136. Because I was a student, the rest of the players said that when the checks came in I could sign my check and put it in the pot. I proceeded to lose all of my money.

When those checks did come, I felt sick as I put my week's worth of pay in the pot. The Grainger brothers sent turkeys to each of us as a Christmas gift. I was so mad that I took that turkey to our apartment and shoved it into the freezer as hard as I could. I drove home to spend Christmas with my family and it was a sad, sad ride. What was I going to tell them? Hi, everyone. Say hello to the Grinch?

When we returned to our apartment at Spartan Village, our apartment stunk like someone or something had died there. Apparently, when I body slammed that turkey into the ice box, I had also broken the freezer.

That was it for me and gambling. In a way, that $136 loss probably saved me a fortune over the years.

I did keep gambling in other ways, however. For example, I kept screwing up in East Lansing. I was a junior and was taking a wrestling class required for physical education majors. I loved it. The class was taught by Fendley Collins, the varsity wrestling coach. Wrestling came naturally to me. Coach Collins would teach us a couple of holds and then we would wrestle for the rest of the hour. Our final exam was a tournament. I won my weight class with ease. But as fate would have it, a good friend and a senior on the MSU football team named Franny O'Brien had missed a lot of classes, and wrestling was one of them. Graduation loomed for him, and Franny was begging Coach Collins for a passing grade. Coach Collins told him that if he could beat me, he would pass.

That was the first match I ever tossed. I let Franny beat me and it made Coach Collins furious. He told me that if that was the way I wanted to play it, he would give Franny my grade and I would get his. That's right, I flunked. That made me ineligible to play football my junior year. Franny went on to play for the Cleveland Browns, Washington Redskins, and Pittsburgh Steelers, and I went on to repeat wrestling class.

By this point, you have to be wondering how I ever graduated from Michigan State. I have asked myself the same question many times. God obviously had a plan for me, even if plans are sometimes covered with mud from an ROTC parade field.

I did make the dean's list. Unfortunately, it wasn't the list for academic achievers. Instead, I was put on academic probation. Then I was put on strict probation.

Enter Roy Niemeyer, a great man who was my class advisor. He knew something was wrong with me, but he also knew it had nothing to do with intelligence. He knew I was smart enough, I just had problems processing information in the usual way. Roy went well out of his way to convince some of my professors to give me oral exams rather than written ones. I have always had a great memory. Plus, once my tongue had finally healed, I loved to talk.

I took a part-time job at the State of Michigan Boys Vocational School, aka reform school, in Lansing. The facility provided great practical training for future teachers and coaches.

I interviewed for the position with Paul Spata, the school's athletic director. He walked me through the field house just as the boys were lining up to go to their next class. As we walked past them I heard some chattering. I knew what was happening, and then out of nowhere someone yelled, "Moose, is that you? What did they get you for?" I waved to the guys and they went nuts. I figured that little exchange had blown my chances at a job.

Back in his office, Paul broke into a big smile as he told me I had the job. He said that a lot of very good people had applied for the position, and that I got the job *because* of my background. He thought I could relate better to the residents, aka inmates, better than some of the button-down-collar types he had been interviewing.

I became a recreation instructor at the school. That allowed me the opportunity be a football and wrestling coach. I really enjoyed working with the guys. We had a great field house, complete with a pool, wrestling and boxing rooms, and a dirt arena the size of a football field, plus a hardwood basketball court smack-dab in the middle.

Things were certainly never dull at the vocational school. For one, the boys were always trying to escape. Trouble was, that only amounted to more trouble for them. We had the option of either chasing the boys or letting the cops catch them later. There were no fences or barbed wire. I always chose option A; I did everything I could to keep them from getting into more trouble.

Paul told me not to hit any of the students unless it was absolutely necessary. But he followed up that advice with a postscript: if it *was* necessary to hit someone, make sure you really lay him out. There was no such thing as a love tap. If I had to drill someone, I would never have to do it again because word would get out. The opposite was also true. Wimps need not apply for that job.

One day we were playing flag football on a field next to the field house. A manhole cover situated in the middle of that field started to move. Soon, up popped a head. Rather than engaging in an impromptu version of Whack-A-Mole, I grabbed the kid. He could not have been more shocked.

Another time, we were playing half-court basketball. There were about eight players per team, and if the other team took a shot and missed, you could just rebound the ball and shoot it yourself. With all of those players on half a court, things got predictably physical. James Naismith, meet George Halas. As the game went on, I tied up the ball with this new inmate. He was about 6'3" and 240 pounds, and not more than a couple of ounces were baby fat. As I pulled the ball away, this guy balled his fist and popped me a good one. He squared off to fight. Everybody started reacting and I knew that this could get out of hand in a hurry. Without hesitation, I slugged him and followed that with a shot right to the jaw. For good measure, I hit him one more time as he was going down for the count. We never had another problem after that. Word got around quickly, and that was without the benefit of any social media. Only birds did tweeting back in those days.

I did have another situation at the school. The basketball court had a three-foot-high net around its edge to keep the basketballs off the dirt floor. There were signs every 10 feet or so warning people not to jump the net. The rule was simple; if anyone chose to ignore it, they had to run five laps around the field house.

One of the players jumped over the net anyway, and I knew right away that this young man had a real problem of some sort. His eyes were blazing. I walked over and asked him what was wrong, and he took a wild swing that just missed me. As he wound up for a second swing, I snatched him and threw him over my shoulder. I assumed he had been in reform school long enough to know he shouldn't mess with me. He was squirming and kicking, but I had a good hold of him. I just wanted to get him to the office so we could talk without getting the rest of the boys worked up.

Instead, he surprised me by reaching down and squeezing my testicles. It was not a gentle caress, either. Sorry Bob Barker, but since I was not quite ready to be spayed or neutered, I flipped him to the ground with extreme malice. He then ran to the weightlifting equipment and picked up a seven-foot metal bar as a weapon. Things were getting out of hand in a hurry. There were more than 100 young men in the field house and the last thing I wanted was a riot on my hands.

I walked toward the boy, staring him directly in the eye. I was hoping to intimidate him using the same tactic I wound up using many times as a professional wrestler. Everybody was hollering at him to put down the bar, that Coach Myers was going to kill him. As I got closer, he realized a metal bar that weighed 25 pounds was probably not an optimal weapon. He sprinted to the other side of the field house and grabbed a starting block from the track. He slipped off the T portion and now had the perfect weapon: a pipe with a spiked block on the end of it. Even though the situation was getting very dangerous, I continued to walk toward him. I knew I could not show any fear. The students got very quiet. As luck would have it, my intimidation tactic worked and he dropped the starting block. As I started walking him toward the office, he took yet another swing at me. I opted for the tough love approach and decked him, all the while dragging him into the office. I felt bad for the young man when I found out that he was an epileptic who was sometimes prone to violence.

Violence can be a constructive thing, especially when it is prompted by a hiked football or occurs on the wrestling mat. I had a chance to be an assistant coach for both the football and wrestling teams at the school. We were blessed to have some very natural athletes, although their level of discipline sometimes mirrored the behavior found in *Lord of the Flies*. A good share of our top athletes were African American. We played mostly schools in farming communities, and the only brown and black skin most of those boys had ever seen before mooed or whinnied. Intimidation and athleticism were definitely in our favor. The kids were at the school for six months and then released, but they would cry if they were released in the middle of football season. After all, they were having the most success they had ever experienced. Unfortunately, most of them went back to their old environments and found the same old problems. They turned into repeat offenders and returned to our facility. The second time around, they were often much more difficult to deal with.

In a lot of ways, I could relate to these young men. Most of them had real problems in school, just like I did. Some of them also had learning disabilities. Others just had no one who cared about them. Thank goodness that was not a part of my plight, too.

The state of Michigan was in the process of moving the school to a new location near Whitmore Lake and changing its name to the Boys Training School. I was offered a job at the new facility, earning $9,000 per year. I chose to take a teaching job back in Madison Heights at less than half that amount. I wanted to work with young people *before* they wound up in an institution.

My mom and dad were very proud of me on graduation day at Michigan State. Believe it or not, I went on to earn a masters degree and even progressed a few hours beyond that in college.

Something I learned at Michigan State and tried to pass on during my own career as a teacher and coach is that learning is not done only in the classroom. Wisdom is not something gathered only during lectures. If it was not for the wisdom of my advisor, Roy Niemeyer, only the Lord knows what I would be doing today.

It probably would not be writing a book. It might not have been even reading a book.

CHAPTER 5

Who Said You Can't Go Home(room) Again?

Author Thomas Wolfe had it all wrong when he said you can't go home again. I guess I proved him wrong. I did go home again. I went into the teachers' lounge. I went to the principal's office, into the gymnasium, and generally anywhere I felt like going.

Quite honestly, my intention was never to go back to Madison Heights to work as a teacher and a coach. But that is exactly what I did.

Before I graduated from college, I had plans to head to a small community in northern Michigan where I could make a name for myself as a teacher and a coach. I was not sure where, I just knew I was going to point my car north and drive. I'm neither Lewis nor Clark, but I wanted to set off on my own and discover a place where nobody knew who Jim Myers was.

But Roy Niemeyer, my advisor at Michigan State, thought that would be a horrible idea. He thought it was important that I returned home to set the record straight. By then, my dyslexia had been diagnosed and I knew I was not dumb. It was time to make amends with the teachers, the administrators, and mostly, with myself.

The idea boggled my mind, to be honest with you. Jim Myers in the teachers' lounge? The same kid who spent his high school career bouncing between the gym and wood shop?

I agreed to go back home for a couple of years before moving on. At least, that was the original plan. That couple of years turned into several decades.

My mom was on the school board, and truth be told, that probably did not hurt my candidacy. But I applied directly to Foster Wilkinson, who was the superintendent. He hired me as a teacher and coach.

When I was a student in high school, the district had hired Gerald Bush, a former prison warden, to be the principal. That is not as unusual as it seems. The student body definitely needed more discipline. Madison High was no pinky-up private school. There was no "Academy" trailing the name.

Things did not work out for Bush as principal, so they bumped him up to assistant superintendent. I don't want to say it was an example of the Peter Principle, because his name was Gerald.

Bush was the assistant superintendent when I was hired. One day he came into the teachers' lounge and sarcastically said to me, "Gee, I don't know how you got hired here." I looked right back at him and replied that my mother was on the school board, but what I could not figure out is how *he* had gotten a job in Madison. That really ticked him off.

I quickly discovered that even as a teacher I did not feel comfortable in the teachers' lounge. When you are a student, the door to the teachers' lounge takes on almost mystical properties. Once a teacher goes in, he or she will not be seen for the longest time. Was there a hot tub inside? Was there an open bar serving martinis and Rob Roys? Was there a television set or a disco ball or a buffet boasting meats, cheeses, and dips?

I found out that there were definitely dips behind the door of the teachers' lounge, but they were of the two-legged variety. One day, a couple of teachers were talking about a boy who happened to be on my track team. One said that the boy came into her class chewing gum and she ordered him to get rid of it, so he went up and spit the gum in the trash can. She was appalled by that method of disposal and promised to flunk him. The other teacher said that the same kid was a borderline student in her class, and that she would flunk him, too. This was more than I could handle. I said, "Wait a minute, did you just say that he is going to fail two classes because he did not know how to properly dispose of his chewing gum?" I told them I thought it was ridiculous to flunk a student because he did not properly dispose of his gum, and they just looked at me like I was crazy.

I always had a lot of sympathy for students, especially the troubled ones, because of my own experiences in school. I knew what it was like to be on the edge, just like this young man was. To hear a couple of teachers making decisions like that for such a petty reason was appalling to me.

Sure, there were some teachers who were equally appalled that I was now among their ranks. I could not blame them. Remember, just a few years earlier I had been loitering at the bottom of the grade curve. Amazingly, one of the teachers who probably should have been hardest on me became a dear friend. His name was Mr. Rowe, and he took me under his wing. He showed me things like the best way to fill out a grade book and other necessary aspects of the job. He was a disciplinarian, and while I certainly appreciated that trait as a teacher, I think my appreciation level was a little lacking when I was a student.

I don't remember if I ever had Mr. Rowe as a teacher, but I am certain I gave him some grief. Rules did not ride shotgun with me when I was in school. It was all a product of the frustration I found in the classroom. Mr. Rowe became so helpful to me as a teacher that it almost broke my heart.

I knew that coaching would never break my heart. After all, nearly all of my success in school had come through athletics. I had two coaches in high school, and they both coached two sports. Carl Baker was my track and basketball coach, while Don Scott coached football and baseball. They knew my academic challenges, and they provided the foundation for my successes in athletics. I lettered in four sports every year, and the coaches were the guys who gave me an opportunity.

I had gotten my first taste of coaching back when I was still a student. I managed a recreation department baseball team the summer before my senior year. The department itself was run by Chuck Skinner, another Madison High grad, who was probably six years older than me. Chuck started the baseball league, and he was one of the other coaches. The league championship came down to my team against Chuck's team. Before that series started, I got the parents to put up some money and I bought some uniforms at the old Griswold's sporting goods store in Detroit. We were the first team in Madison Heights to wear uniforms, and I am sure Chuck did not like it.

It was a best-of-five series, and it came down to the fifth game. The game time was scheduled to be 6:00 PM but Chuck decided to change it to 2:00 in the afternoon. Since he was the director of the recreation department, he could do that. Who could I complain to?

I was working construction, and I did not know anything about the change, so my mom came to the construction site to tell me. I hustled to the field wearing my work clothes. We won the game.

Chuck became one of the best high school football coaches in Michigan. He turned around programs at Hazel Park High School and

Birmingham Seaholm High School, so beating him in anything was a thrill, even back when we were kids. Having success with that baseball team helped me find my niche.

I was certainly smart enough to realize that in order to coach, I also had to teach. Even so, when I went back to Madison Heights as a teacher, I still struggled with spelling. I learned to compensate quickly. Spelling was a subject taught in homeroom. Typically, those lessons took place right after I took attendance. I quickly identified two of the smartest seventh graders in homeroom. They became the spelling instructors, and that is the way I handled it. We had 10 spelling words per week, and the students were responsible for learning the new words. Year after year, I would identify the best spellers in homeroom and designate them the instructors.

I was a physical education and health teacher. I was lucky to have some great professors at Michigan State. Therefore, I did not just walk into the gym, roll out a ball, and shout "Dodgeball!" We worked on body alignment. We performed specialized exercises. We divided into groups and marched. I taught skills in sports like volleyball, baseball, and wrestling. In fact, it was through gym class that we started the school wrestling program. We instituted an intramural program so that kids could compete after school.

Coaching is what I believe God put me on earth to do, even more so than yanking hidden objects out of my wrestling trunks. I turned down a fortune by returning to Madison High every fall for years. I believed in what I was doing and that it was best thing for the kids and the best thing for me.

Teaching is about values and doing the right thing. When I started teaching there would be a certain group of kids who would not participate in gym class. They were just biding time until they were old enough to drop out. They were a pain in the neck and tried to bully the other kids. While I would continually try to get them to dress for gym and get to know them as individuals, I did not bend to their values in the slightest. Even with all of my problems in school, I had always tried to participate. These kids had dropped out mentally before they were physically allowed to do it.

After my second year of teaching, I was up for tenure. Bob Liike was principal of the junior high school. He would later become superintendent. Bob told me that even though I was doing great, he was not recommending me for tenure because I lacked confidence. I was livid; how could I coach and teach and not have confidence? While I eventually did get tenure, I stayed mad for a while. Looking back, Bob was right. My confidence had always been gained from athletics, and that continued as an adult. Only instead of hunkering down on the football field or setting up shop in the lane on the basketball court, I was raging about the wrestling ring in front of thousands of fans. The more I wrestled and the more successful I became, the more I gained confidence. That confidence showed not just in places like Madison Square Garden or the Boston Garden, but also in front of the classroom.

I was blessed but not even smart enough yet to thank God for those blessings. My first teaching job was at Wilkinson Junior High and I was there for two years, from 1961 to 1963. I had a bunch of really great kids both in my classes and on my teams. My football teams were undefeated, and so were my track teams.

A potential new problem was looming, however. Unlike the reform school, the junior high meant there were parents to deal with. My first run-in was over getting dressed for gym class. Can you imagine that? I wanted everyone to wear shorts and T-shirts, and there was no way I was going to allow blue jeans and shoes with pointed toes.

Another point of contention was the fact that I was making $4,300 a year teaching and coaching. With a wife, two children, and another one on the way, we were strapped for cash. Our budget was so thin it was almost anorexic. I supplemented the income by umpiring youth baseball games. I worked Wednesday night recreation dances. I taught driver's education. I delivered flowers. We were still in dire straits.

It was time to search for another source of income.

My extracurricular options were limited because I was already teaching, coaching, and, occasionally, parenting. I knew I was no model. Abercrombie & Fitch never called. They did not need me to wriggle into their briefs or model their blue jeans. Thanks goodness, because if they had, I probably never would have made a dime in professional wrestling.

You've seen those Abercrombie & Fitch models, right? There's more hair on any self-respecting peach than on their chests. And, heaven forbid, back hair? Somebody call the suicide hotline. Any one of those models would have to be talked off a ledge if they spotted even one aberrant follicle sprouting anywhere north of the body's Mason-Dixon Line.

But I digress. Let's get back to square one—or, if you prefer, into the squared circle. It was 1962, and the income of a typical junior high school teacher was hardly bringing in ground beef, let alone beef Wellington.

I took a quick inventory of my qualifications and schedule. I was a big, brawny guy. I was intelligent enough, but being a brain surgeon was not an option. How about working as a bouncer?

I figured I would go right to the potential job source, so I went bar-hopping with my good friend, David Pierce. I did not grab a fistful of résumés. I just made a big, beefy fist and figured I would let it speak for itself. I had the menacing face of a cop before his first cup of coffee and glazed doughnut. I had always been an athlete. I'd been in my share of fights. What else would a bar be looking for? The hours were right. I'd be done teaching. I'd be done coaching. I would be working nights.

So David and I went out drinking. The more we drank, the more qualified I became. Unfortunately, nursing longnecks did not get me any closer to a job as a bouncer. Dave was a huge wrestling fan and often told me I should become a wrestler. I always laughed him off because I thought professional wrestling was phony. Mix a carnival barker with a politician, add a couple of biceps, and *voilà!* But then Dave told me he had read how much money Walter "Killer" Kowalski made wrestling in one night, and that caught my interest. A steady supply of diapers and baby food did not come cheaply.

After a few more bars and a few more beers, I found myself calling a local wrestling promoter at 1:30 AM. His name was Bert Ruby, and Dave and I had found his number in the phone book. I knew it was a little late to be calling anyone, especially a potential employer, but alcohol and social graces do not always sling an arm around one another's shoulders. I am absolutely certain I woke him up, but I told him I wanted to be a wrestler. To my shock, he did not let loose a string of profanities. Instead, he invited me over to his house the next day after school.

The following afternoon, I found myself standing at Bert's front door in Oak Park, another suburb of Detroit, which was probably 10 minutes away from Madison Heights. For some reason, I was sweaty-palms nervous, like a kid going to pick up his prom date. I had no idea what to expect.

He opened the door, took one look at me, and said, "Beautiful." I was a bit taken aback by that reaction. After I had said hello to his wife, his sons, and his mother-in-law, we excused ourselves and moved into his office for a private meeting. We talked about my background as an athlete and a teacher. He asked me what I knew about the professional wrestling business. I was honest and told him I did not know anything at all about it, that I just needed a job. That's when Bert asked me to remove my jacket, shirt, and tie. I had been in my share of job interviews, but this was a first. If he said anything about my pants, I'd already decided I was out of there. He went bananas when he saw I had a thick torso that was covered in body hair. How much body hair do I have? Let's just say the typical Yeti would be envious. If they did Brazilian waxes on backs and chests, it would have taken five or six Brazilians to tackle this chore. Bert could not have been more excited. He kept telling me how important it was that a wrestler look strong.

Since I was a teacher, it was decided that I should wear a mask. I guess that was a smart decision since the principal, the superintendent, and the school board probably would not have seen the value in a teacher and coach running around in tights and boots in a wrestling ring. I was going to be called the Student, since I was just learning the wrestling business.

The plan was to train with Gino Brito in a gym situated in the basement of a church in Windsor, Ontario. The Canadian city is located directly across the Detroit River from the Motor City. The fact that a bunch of professional wrestlers worked out in a church proved to me that yes, the Lord works in mysterious ways, and yes, He has a real sense of humor. The gym consisted of a ring, a few weights, and a set of parallel bars.

On my first day there, Gino was nowhere to be found, but four other wrestlers were waiting for me. Very quickly, their intention was clear: they were going to give the new recruit a strenuous conditioning workout, and after they had worn me out, they would take turns kicking my asterisk all over the ring. Only that blueprint got a little smudged, mostly by their own sweat. First, I was in very good shape, probably in much better shape than they were. Second, if there was an aptitude test given in high school, fighting would've been pretty darn close to my chosen avocation. I was good at it, and that quickly became apparent to the other wrestlers in the gym that day. In their defense, they were not trying to be mean; they were just trying to make sure I was serious about wrestling. The idea had always been that if a new recruit came back to the gym after taking a thrashing on the first day, he was serious about wrestling.

Well, the thrashee became the thrasher.

Therein lay another problem. The whole idea of getting into wrestling was to supplement my income, not deplete it. In order to get to the gym in Windsor, I had to take the Detroit-to-Windsor tunnel. A one-way trip cost 25 cents—and while that might not seem like much, there was no such thing as pocket change for me in those days. Pat and I were struggling, and a package of Hostess Twinkies might as well have been a wedding cake for the royals. Fifty cents twice a week for five months of training equaled a lot more than I had bargained for.

In fact, Pat laughed when I came home that first afternoon from Oak Park. She said I would never make enough money in professional wrestling to pay the tolls.

A handful of months and no matches later, I began to fear that she was correct.

Thankfully, we were both wrong. Eventually, that first match arrived, and it was time for the Student to get his wrestling uniform. Now came the hard part. Where does one find pro wrestling gear? Someone told me to buy a woman's girdle and make my own mask, which was more of a hood. I did just that, and I must tell you that I wish I had saved it. No one would believe what my first wrestling mask looked like. What a piece of wrestling history! This thing was about two sizes too small. I had cut out ear holes so that I could hear what my opponents were saying. It was so tight that my eyes bulged and my lips stuck out like Angelina Jolie's. I had also done a poor job of dyeing it red. I ordered my wrestling uniform from a high school athletic salesman named Tommy Christopher. It consisted of a red shirt, red trunks, and a red leotard. I guess you might say I looked like Not-So-Little Red Riding Hood. I ordered a red cap and gown from the company that supplied Madison High School's graduates. I have my first wrestling picture taken on the Madison High stage standing behind a podium. The picture was taken by a fellow physical education teacher Carolyn Strumble.

I called Bert and told him I was ready for my first pro wrestling match. He told me I was booked for Thursday night at the Kalamazoo, Michigan, Armory at 7:30 PM. Then Bert gave me directions to the Eddystone Hotel on Cass Avenue in downtown Detroit. I was told to go to the Motor City Wrestling office on the fifth floor, where I would find someone to drive me to Kalamazoo.

Ah, the old Eddystone Hotel, *old* being the operative word. As I came through the Eddystone's revolving door, I was enveloped in a musty smell. The man behind the front desk wasn't a bell boy, he was a crypt keeper. It looked as if rigor mortis had already set in. He just sat there with this blank expression on his face, reading the sports section from the *Detroit Times*. He should have been scanning the obituaries, looking for his own name.

To the right of the front desk were large, arched doors. I peeked inside the room behind them and my nostrils were assaulted by the stench of stale beer and cigarette smoke. There was a long bar and two pockmarked pool tables. It was 4:30 in the afternoon and the place was crowded. A woman known as Little Bit was the head honcho. She had about 30 hookers who worked out of the hotel. Even bed bugs hesitated before checking into the Eddystone. It was a strange environment. There was a lot of conversation between the wrestlers and the girls, but that is as far as it went.

When I got out on the fifth floor, the elevator doors opened to one large suite. There was a hulking desk at one end of the room where four businessmen sat playing poker. No one looked my way. The one player who stood out was dressed in a navy blue silk suit with a blue star-sapphire ring on his pinkie finger. Boy, was I impressed. I made it a goal to have one of those sapphire pinkie rings someday.

Also in the room was a circle of chairs filled with huge bodies. Only a couple of those guys looked up. I felt totally out of place, but $50 for one night's work was still the hook, so there I stood. Finally, Gino looked up and came over to greet me with a whisper. He explained that we were waiting for a couple more wrestlers and then we would split into groups of four and head for the Kalamazoo Armory.

Heels (bad guys) and babyfaces (good guys) rode in separate cars. Gino told me that I was a heel, so I would not be riding with him. Wow, what a way to go to my first wrestling show as a participant! I had never even been to a wrestling show before.

The drive west on I-94 was strange. Nobody said a word. I did not expect a bunch of geniuses, but I figured there would be some conversation. I must say that it was a bit intimidating. I had no idea what to expect, but I was relieved when Bert Ruby showed up in Kalamazoo with a smile. That was the first smile that I had seen all day.

Bert called 350-pound Klondike Bill and me into the shower (that is where we used to talk business). Bert told Klondike Bill that this was my first match. Bert suggested that we have a half-shoot and that I would grab a fall after about 10 minutes. After about seven minutes in the ring, we were both really sucking air. Bill and I went about 12 minutes and I got paid $25. The money is what made the day.

The return trip to Detroit was very different. Some of the experienced wrestlers critiqued my performance. Most were pretty complimentary. The silent act was over and now it was like a coffee klatch—only we were not drinking coffee. After a short drive, I experienced my first bologna blowout. It consisted of a six-pack of beer, potato chips, a loaf of bread, mustard, and a pound of bologna. Wheaties might be the breakfast of champions, but bologna and Wonder Bread was the dinner of heels and babyfaces.

The conversation was mostly about wrestling. There was some other guy talk sprinkled in, too. As we cruised back to Detroit, whenever a guy finished a beer, he leaned out an open window and launched the bottle at a road sign. It was my introduction to a new sport called "sign tossing." Geez, I felt like one of the boys already.

When we arrived back at the Eddystone, I got another professional wrestling lesson. It was time to pony up for the transportation costs. The driver, Lou Klein, collected 2 cents per mile. The trip had been 180 miles. The transportation cost, plus bologna, chips, beer, and mustard, meant I had made $16 on my first night as a professional wrestler. Our new baby would hardly be born with a silver spoon in his mouth. Heck, he might not even get a mouthful of mashed carrots.

That night marked not only the beginning of a new income source; it was also the start of a Sybil-like existence that went on for years. By day, I was a conservative, well-grounded husband, father, teacher, and coach. By night, I was the Student, a man who would eventually become the Animal. I became a teacher in the fall of 1961 and I would retire from that job in January 1986. There was a whole lot of split personality during that time.

By far the hardest part of my existence was juggling the different lifestyles of my two occupations. There aren't many action figures made of high school teachers and coaches, and honestly, that is too bad.

I'd go from wrestling in front of thousands of people to standing in front of a high school football team within 24 hours. I'd be smack-dab in the middle of a party in New York City or Boston, and 24 hours later, I'd be in the locker room at Madison High or in the teachers' lounge.

Now *that* is a sudden change. Pat was always right there to help me. She had a familiar saying that became very important to me: "Now we must get Jim out of the box and put George in the box."

CHAPTER 6

Pittsburgh: The Steele City

It's not easy being green. Who said that first, Kermit the Frog or George "the Animal" Steele? My green tongue happened entirely by accident. I was scheduled to do an interview on Channel 11 in Pittsburgh, and I had been chewing Clorets gum. Unbeknownst to me, the mint gum had turned my tongue green. Well, the viewers loved it, and from then on, I had to have a tongue the shade of a bullfrog's rear end. It became my trademark.

My big break in wrestling came when Bruno Sammartino, the WWWF champion, had a match at Detroit's Cobo Arena with Bulldog Brower. Sammartino saw me wrestling and asked if I wanted to work in Pittsburgh. They did not want a masked man in Pittsburgh, so the Student became George Steele.

It was a huge break. Up until that point, I had never really been anywhere else to wrestle. My road trips were literally that: hop in the car and drive to places like Kalamazoo or Muskegon or Toledo; wrestle for $50 or $100; stop at the store on the way back for some bread, bologna, and beer; and get home in the early morning hours. Catch a few winks and punch in at school as a teacher and coach.

The offer from Sammartino came at a great time, too. The wrestling business in Detroit was changing. Gary Hart and I had been with promoter Bert Ruby, but when the Sheik came into town, he brought in all of these other guys. All of a sudden, Gary and I were looked upon as second-class citizens. One person in particular, Lord Athol Layton, really looked down his nose at us. He was an Englishman and played the part of royalty all too well. He obviously thought his wrestling garb did not stink. Layton did not want anything to do with us.

He was a real pain in the butt, and ironically, that turned into a big break for us. The Sheik had a horrible case of hemorrhoids and needed surgery. So, Gary Hart was scheduled for a match against Lord Layton at Cobo. I also got on the card and we drew really well.

Soon enough, Bruno Sammartino came to Detroit, and soon enough, I went to Pittsburgh.

It was a very exciting time. I had never flown anywhere to wrestle before. On the airport shuttle to the hotel, we went into the Liberty Tunnels, which are also known as the Liberty Tubes. The Tubes bored right through Mt. Washington and allowed motorists to cruise between the South Hills and the city.

Coming out of the Tubes I was greeted with a magnificent view of the city. I was enthralled. Welcome to the Steel City. To me it was Shangri La, Utopia, and the Garden of Eden wrapped into one, with some ice-cold beer and a 24-ounce sirloin thrown in. I was greeted by what is called the Golden Triangle. A glorious Hilton Hotel was part of the panorama. From there we got on the Liberty Bridge, crossing the Monongahela River.

I was going out of town to wrestle, and I had no idea at the time how much my life would change. Good-bye bologna, hello prime rib and lobster.

When I got to the lobby of the hotel, I ran into Reginald Lisowski, also known as the Crusher. He was frequently Dick the Bruiser's tag team partner. He did not know me from Rock Hudson, but I had seen him at wrestling shows in Detroit. We chatted for a while.

Ironically, my first match in Pittsburgh was against Gino Brito, who had taught me how to wrestle in that small gym in the church's basement back in Windsor. On the same card that night, Batman and Bruno Sammartino defeated Dr. Bill Miller and Crusher Cortez.

The following day was a TV match promoted by Rudy Miller and Ace Freeman. Since I did not have a manager in those days, I did all my own talking. There were none of the monosyllabic, drool-ridden promos that would come later. People could understand me without benefit of a translator and a tranquilizer gun. I was also very serious about wrestling. I did not do all the crazy stuff I later became known for. I used actual wrestling holds and I was pretty vicious. Nobody enjoyed being in the wrestling ring with me. In fact, there were some people who hated wrestling me, but as I got more popular with the fans, they quickly changed their tune.

Main events in Pittsburgh paid $1,200, which was some pretty good money back then. By comparison, guys in the NFL were making $7,000 or $8,000 per season, and I was pulling in slightly more than $4,000 per year as a teacher and a coach.

After a couple of tag team bouts, I was wrestling against Sammartino for the WWWF title. The Pittsburgh Civic Arena was rocking with fans who just could not get enough of the wild brawls that I was having with Bruno.

Not all of the wild brawls in Pittsburgh were sanctioned. After matches, I would often go to an after-hours bar and restaurant located across the street from our rooms at the Roosevelt Hotel. I would stop there to grab a meal late at night because nothing else was open. I had a great relationship with the staff in that joint. Everybody was friendly, and there was never any trouble there.

Until the late night from hell.

There were three or four customers in the place having a few drinks. I was sitting alone, enjoying a steak and a beer. What I did not know is that a group of lowlifes had caused a ruckus the night before and that nine of these jerks had tried to come back again earlier in the evening. The doorman had only let two of the druggies in—to find a friend.

Or so they said.

Those two made Charles Manson look well groomed. As they came in, one of them took a swing at a guy sitting by the entrance. A fight broke out. I had been around more than a few bar fights in my time, and they were usually over in under a minute. Well, this one went on and on.

Finally, enough was enough. I had at least half a sirloin and three-quarters of a beer to attend to and these guys who looked like they had mange were disturbing my peace.

I walked over, grabbed one of the druggies, and treated him like a wet umbrella. I stuffed him in a closet.

I told him to relax, that this was a friendly place. But as I was standing there trying to reason with him, his partner passed him a piece over my shoulder. The next thing I realized, I was on the wrong end of a *Dirty Harry* confrontation. I was the punk, and he was asking me if I felt lucky. I didn't bother replying; instead, I smacked him and he dropped the gun on the floor of the closet.

I started to weigh my options, and there were not a lot of them. While I was never one to leave behind even a small morsel of food, I opted to get out of Dodge. What I didn't realize was that both Tombstone and the O.K. Corral were waiting out in the street.

The seven guys who could not get into the bar were still waiting outside. Unknowingly, I shouted at them to run because there was a crazy guy with a gun inside. Suddenly, the guy with the gun came bursting out of the bar shouting, "Get that bald-headed bastard!"

Now, I have my limits, and I took great offense at that. While I was certainly bald-headed, I really am not 100 percent bastard. At times 90 or 95 percent, but never pure, unadulterated bastard. These guys were not about to debate the point. I got hit with a heavy chain and dropped to my knees. The guy with the gun slapped me across the face with it. I was beaten mercilessly. I was kicked around in Lou Groza fashion. I was cut numerous times with a razor. It was a good thing Lorena Bobbitt was not in the crowd, or I would have been neutered, too. The doorman just watched because they had a sawed off shotgun held on him. I was later told that I started convulsing like I was ready to move from the sports pages to the obituaries.

Despite the pummeling, I eventually came around. Since it was an after-hours joint, the police were never called. The staff helped me to my hotel room. When I woke up the next morning, it looked like an explosion at the Red Cross. The room was covered in blood.

That afternoon, I went on television with a towel over my head. I was asked if Bruno Sammartino had gotten a hold of me. I took the opportunity to utter a warning: I was from Detroit and I knew how to give out receipts.

I called Pat and told her to prepare the kids to see their dad in bad shape. I even flew home with a towel over my head. I was a mess. My face, while never residing in the pretty category, was horribly cut and bruised. My skin tone for a couple of weeks was black and blue. I couldn't teach or coach for a couple of weeks afterward.

I might have been badly hurt, but I was also livid and intent on revenge. I've never been a pacifist, and I was going to find those guys and wreak some havoc of my own. However, I was told not to get involved, that the police department would handle it in its own way. I could not swear to this, but I heard later that a couple of the guys wound up deceased, a couple more were pounded into serious submission, and all eventually wound up on the wrong side of fate. Apparently, one of the guys that had attacked me was a police informant, and that was how the cops found out who was involved. These were some seriously messed up individuals who got seriously messed up themselves.

Despite looking like Chuck Wepner after his whupping by Muhammad Ali, I still loved Pittsburgh. Outside of the Detroit area and Michigan, it was where I got my first opportunity to make some real money in wrestling.

There was another place near the Roosevelt Hotel that was a little fancier. It was called Frenchy's Restaurant, and their fare was slightly upscale, especially for a guy who dined regularly on the stuffing from turnbuckles and Clorets gum. They catered to an upper-crust crowd, and nobody ever accused me of being high society. If I had a finger raised, it was only because I had broken it in a match.

Frenchy's was owned by two brothers and their mother, and they treated me like family. The brothers were huge wrestling fans and they always saved a large round table in the middle of the dining room for us wrestlers. They put out a huge salad bowl and pasta and served us family style. Everything was there to eat communally except for our entrees, which we ordered individually.

I was usually late on the Civic Arena's wrestling card. I got to Frenchy's one night and the restaurant was already packed with folks who had come from a nearby theater. I am not talking about the theater where you watched John Wayne or Charles Bronson and shoveled popcorn down your gullet. These people had come from a play and were dressed up. You could hear a buzz as I walked through the dining room. Obviously I was not part of the tuxedo crowd. My place was already set so I proceeded to put some salad in my bowl and pasta on my plate. One of the other wrestlers asked if I'd like his leftover steak. I said sure, and put that on my plate, too.

There was a lady from the theater group sitting at one of the tables next to us. She looked a little bit like Joan Rivers before Joan was in that head-on collision with the Botox truck. I did not know if she had a clue who we were or if she was just being smart, but she held up her plate with a two-pound lobster falling off its sides and said, "I suppose you would like my lobster, too." So, I reached over and snatched the lobster off the lady's plate. I broke off the tail, put it on my plate, and returned the carcass to her. She started to scream that I had stolen her lobster. Mondi, one of the brothers who owned Frenchy's, doubled over in laughter. He told her she had just offered her lobster to George "the Animal" Steele.

That wasn't enough to make the lady happy, so I bought her a drink, Mondi brought her another lobster, and we all had a great laugh.

There was something about nightspots, Pittsburgh, and George "the Animal" Steele that produced scripts that were hard to imagine, much less believe.

One night I literally brought the house down in McKeesport, which is not too far outside of Pittsburgh. We had a show there and one of the referees was Emil Britko, a former boxer and a fun guy. He was also the doorman at a rough bar in the Hill district. Emil really wanted us to stop in and have a drink, and we decided to oblige.

The place was great and full of a lot of fun people. Wrestling was hot in Pittsburgh, and we were recognized everywhere we went. Emil's place was no exception. Everyone was very decent and respectful, except for one guy. He wanted to ask me a question. I told him to keep it simple. He said he was 6'1" and 230 pounds and he asked if I thought I could body slam him. I just told him it was neither the time nor place for that.

Cowed, he went back to his table, proceeded to down a couple beers, and then he was back. The alcohol made him a little more adamant. He said that wrestling was fake and there was no way that I could ever body slam him. Emil saw what was going on and told the guy to go back to his table and knock it off.

The restrooms were upstairs. There was also a large dance floor at the top of the stairs, but it was dark on this particular night. When I went to the john, the same guy was standing in the dark in the middle of the dance floor. I guessed he did not want to waltz and I was right. He said menacingly that it was just the two of us and he wanted to see if I could slam him.

I figured I might as well make this guy's wish come true. I told him to give me his head. He did, and I clamped a front face lock on him that would've taken the jaws of life to get out of. I had his head turned and the side of my forearm in position to put a lot of pressure in just the right place. I came up through the crotch with enough force to pick Andre the Giant or Wilt Chamberlain off the ground. In one motion I scooped him up and slammed him down in the middle the dance floor. All the big fellow said was, "Wow!"

Suddenly, there was a lot of commotion downstairs. As we headed calmly for the stairway, a crowd was coming the other way, Emil leading the charge. "What the hell happened?" he shouted. In addition to the people who were following him, a huge cloud of dust was rising up from the bar. Emil told me the ceiling had come down thanks to my little stunt.

When we got down the stairs, I could immediately see that the bar was covered in plaster. Amazingly, nobody had gotten hurt. What was more amazing was what was imprinted on the ceiling. It was a perfect silhouette of the guy that I had just slammed. It looked kind of like a snow angel, at least if this particular angel reeked of alcohol and had a beer belly.

I figured I was in a lot of trouble. I asked the bar owner how much this was going to cost me. He laughed and said all he wanted was an autograph. He got out a stepladder and had me climb up and sign the silhouette as everyone clapped. The fellow who I had slammed drove us back to our hotel. Man, how things have changed. Can you imagine that happening to a wrestler today? First, the police would have been called, and then the lawyers. Or, most likely, it would have been the other way around.

The promoters, Freeman and Miller, had taken me under their wing in Pittsburgh, and they were the ones who convinced me that I shouldn't wear a mask. At first it was strange; not because I have a face that should be emblazoned on the cover of *GQ* magazine, but because I had always hidden the fact I was a wrestler.

But Ace and Rudy did not want me to wear a mask, and neither did the good people who ran the *Studio Wrestling* television show. Their rationale was that people cannot see a guy's facial expressions when he is wearing a mask, and anyone who saw George "the Animal" Steele wrestle knew that my face regularly contorted in Popeye-post-spinach-soufflé fashion. Wrestling without the mask helped me achieve celebrity status in the Pittsburgh area.

The wrestling business was moving from bologna sandwiches to sirloin for me. Still, one thought was always in the back of my mind: how could I really take advantage of this great opportunity?

Enter Ernie Ladd. Ladd came to wrestling from professional football, where it was said he was the biggest, strongest man around. He was 6'9" and 315 pounds, with a 52-inch chest, 39-inch waist, 20-inch biceps, 19-inch neck, 20-inch calves, and size 18D shoes.

Wrestlers were supposed to arrive at venues no later than 7:00 PM on the night of shows. That's what I always did, as prompt as an alarm clock with a type-A personality. Ernie Ladd and I usually stayed at the same hotel. But there was no way Ernie would show up at 7:00. The clock would read 8:00, and the promoter would ask if anyone had seen Ernie. That same question would be repeated in stuttering fashion every 15 minutes or so. By 9:30, the promoter would be sweating like Rodney Dangerfield.

Unlike Rodney, Ernie got plenty of respect. When he would finally show up, the red shag carpet would be rolled out. Ernie Ladd was wrestling royalty. He'd give me a big smile and a wink. Yep, here was real leverage.

Pittsburgh was the start of my transformation and my professional schizophrenia. Do superstars work part-time? Do they blow up volleyballs by day and climb through the ropes at night? Are they vilified by thousands while in the wrestling ring, and then occasionally adored by teenagers in the classroom or on the sideline? I was becoming an occasional superstar thanks to my exposure in the Pittsburgh market. Yet I was still going back to Michigan, where I was a teacher and a coach. It was not always easy shoving George "the Animal" Steele back into the closet and welcoming Jim Myers. Yep, that Sybil feeling was definitely starting to take hold, even though Sybil did not have back hair.

While Pat and the kids would occasionally join me during the summer, Pat never liked the wrestling lifestyle. She liked to keep George totally separate from Jim Myers. But Pat was with me one night in Pittsburgh. We were staying at a Howard Johnson hotel near the airport. After the show, we went into the bar to get a drink, and there were only four or five people there. One guy saw me and followed me into the restroom. He said insulting things to me, but I did not react because my wife was with me. An hour later, this guy took an attacking step toward me as Pat and I were leaving. I gave him a shove and he immediately fell and landed on his head. He started shaking as if he was having a seizure. The police were called and an ambulance came, but the guy's buddies said they'd just take him home. This guy was really drunk. All the while, Pat was screaming and crying. She told me that she just could not stand the lifestyle. That would not be the last time I heard Pat say exactly that, and she was right. That is why wrestling continued to be my part-time job for so long.

Still, wrestling was good to me, and I even talked my brother, Jack, into going with me to Pittsburgh and wrestling as Professor Blood. He lasted one action-packed summer and that was it. Jack was not as excited about the wrestling business as I was, unfortunately.

Jack's education in wrestling did not come off without a hitch. One night in Pittsburgh he twisted his knee. Now, Jack is a tough guy. He was a small-college All-American football player. But his knee hurt so badly he could hardly walk, let alone climb into the wrestling ring. He had a legitimate excuse to sit out a match or two.

That's when I first met a fellow and his wife who were good friends with Dr. Bill Miller, who was a veterinarian and a wrestler. I thought this guy was just a couple of steps this side of Rod Serling, but interesting nonetheless. He was a hypnotist and was forever talking about auras and energy fields.

From what I can remember, this guy said an aura is a field of subtle radiation surrounding a person or object. It could also be called a halo, but since neither my brother nor I was exactly living a lifestyle that befitted that sort of divine designation, I figured that was not the right description. He told us that some people associated colors of their aura with the various personality traits. If that's the case, I would be fascinated to see what shade your typical professional wrestler has riding shotgun with him.

This guy worked on Jack's knee without once touching it. Honest to goodness, I witnessed Jack's knee move and then the pain went away. It was hard to believe. What's next, bending forks and spoons?

Even though it boggled my mind at the time, I eventually forgot about auras. However, that would not be the last time I came into contact with the man who made David Copperfield come off like a carnival act.

Even though Jack was through with wrestling, the future was looking good for me in Pittsburgh. But all of a sudden, I started to hear rumors that Bruno Sammartino was complaining to everyone about my work. I heard that he was saying I did not sell enough and that I was working too stiff.

Well, me being me, I got pissed. I thought that if Bruno had problems with me, then he should have been man enough to tell me to my ugly mug. Screw him; there was no way I was going to call that jerk.

Four months or so later, I got a call from Bruno at school. He began telling me in so many words what I jerk I was. As you can probably imagine, it did not evolve into an intellectual discourse. Soon, he and I were hollering at each other, and not all of our words had more than one syllable. Finally, he told me to shut up and listen for a minute. He said that Vince McMahon was looking for a new heel who had never been in the WWWF. Bruno went on to say that he had told Mr. McMahon that we could draw a lot of money in the Northeast. He also told Mr. McMahon that I was a backstabber. He said I had thanked him to his face, but as soon as I got back to Detroit, I started shooting my big mouth off and knocking the way I got paid.

I then told Bruno what I had heard about him knocking me. It turns out that we had both been fed a line of bull. Misinformation breaks a lot of hearts in wrestling, and it nearly broke Bruno and me apart. In reality, it created a bond that lasted for years. The stage was set for me to meet Mr. McMahon. It was 1968, and Bruno Sammartino had just offered me the opportunity of a lifetime.

CHAPTER 7

It's Quite a Part-Time Job

What started as a part-time job evolved into something that earned me more money than I ever could have imagined. It was certainly much more than I earned a driver's education instructor trying to teach high school kids the difference between a brake pedal and the clutch, between defensive driving and a demolition derby.

I started wrestling to earn extra money because we were financially strapped. Even when I was performing in venues around the world, it still remained a summer job. I was a high school teacher and coach for nine months, and a professional wrestler for three months. That is what my résumé said.

I ultimately made a lot more than $50 per bout. I eventually moved from bologna to prime rib. Instead of the grocery store for some peanut butter and Wonder Bread, I took Pat to the Copacabana.

The Copacabana, often referred to as the Copa, was a famous New York City nightclub. Many entertainers—among them Danny Thomas,

Pat Cooper, and the comedy team of Dean Martin and Jerry Lewis—made their New York debuts there.

It was the place to be, and in 1969 I brought Pat with me to New York. I was wrestling champion Bruno Sammartino for the WWWF title at Madison Square Garden, and I wanted to take Pat to the Copa to see Dionne Warwick's show.

The trouble was, I was a real hayseed. It was like Ma and Pa Walton leaving the mountain and checking in at the Bellagio in Las Vegas. I told Tony Altimore and Lou Albano that I wanted to take Pat to the Copa after my match with Bruno. The great Sicilian tag team and a couple of true-blue New Yorkers, they told me the ins and outs of the Copa. They told me to flash a roll of bills to the maître d' if I wanted to get a table close to the stage. Tony told me to make sure that I picked up the souvenirs, too.

I followed their instructions—at least up to a point. My roll was all $100 bills, and I certainly was not going to hand the maitre d' a hundred bucks. I flashed him the roll; suitably impressed, he took us to a great table. Then I stiffed him. Pat was furious, but remember, I was still a schoolteacher, and a hundred bucks was a hundred bucks. It could have bought a lot more than a good seat in my world.

Dionne Warwick was great, and we had a fabulous time despite the daggers the maitre d' kept shooting our way. When the show ended and it was time to go, I suddenly remembered I had forgotten the souvenirs. I was looking around and there were no programs, no knockers that you'd use to bang on the tables, no Copacabana matches, nothing. Suddenly, I looked at the chairs where another couple had been sitting and there they were. I quickly grabbed them and then, to my eternal embarrassment, the couple came back looking for their souvenirs. I ham-handedly feigned innocence, and they left in disgust. Embarrassment squared—and to top things off, when we went outside, it was pouring rain and we could not find a cab. The hottest spot north of Havana?

Maybe if you measured the temperature of my red face. Barry Manilow can take his lyrics and shove them.

On January 15, 1971, Bruno Sammartino and Dominic DeNucci defeated Baron Mikel Scicluna and George "the Animal" Steele due to disqualification. In that match, I had used a steel chair to knock the Play-Doh out of Sammartino...or at least that was the story. Bruno's shoulder was said to have been severely injured during my assault, and he was told by Louis Civaterese, the ringside doctor in Pittsburgh, to take a few weeks off. Rather than heed that medical advice, Bruno went to New York City and promptly lost the championship to Ivan Koloff. Everyone in Madison Square Garden knew that Bruno was injured, and everyone knew his bum shoulder had my autograph on it.

Koloff's reign was short-lived. Pedro Morales soon pinned the interim WWWF world champion to win the title.

Pedro's ascent was not necessarily good for us heels. He had that knack of whipping fans into a frenzy. If he had been a preacher, he would have been an evangelist. If he had been on television, he would have been selling ShamWows and Ginsu knives. Pedro could get the fans frothing, and that meant they always wanted to help him out. One person's help is another's felony, apparently. Blackjack Mulligan can attest to that. He was attacked from behind and sliced with a straight razor while in the middle of the ring in a match against Pedro at the Boston Garden. He bled like a bad guy in a Quentin Tarantino flick. The doctors needed an extra spool of thread to close the nasty gash. It took 78 stitches. Who had been working security that night, Barney Rubble and Fred Flintstone? All of the top heels were very leery of wrestling Pedro in Boston. So who are you going to call? Not the Ghostbusters, but George "the Animal" Steele.

Mr. McMahon was very concerned about the heat getting out of control and about my safety. He did not make the trip to Boston very often, but he came to the Garden for this show to make sure the security was ready. I am not sure what more he could have done. I always went to and from the ring like somebody who was waiting to be fitted for a straitjacket. I was wild and crazy—and it was done for a purpose. It intimidated the fans and gave me what I called the "fear factor." Most times, rather than running at me, the fans would run the other way. That is exactly what I intended, but Mr. McMahon warned me not do it this time. To be safe, he told me to walk to the ring like a sane individual.

Even though I loved and respected Mr. McMahon, I got mighty ticked off at him during my enforced stroll back to the locker room after my match with Pedro. I got hit with everything from cups of beer to high heels, umbrellas to a walking cane or two. I had somehow managed to enrage even the elderly and the handicapped in the Hispanic community. When I got close to the locker room, I glanced at a mirror and I was covered in blood. Either that, or a can of Campbell's tomato soup had exploded on my head—and there was no hint of oyster crackers anywhere in the neighborhood. I told Mr. McMahon that night that while he might be a great promoter, I would get to and from the ring in my own way. The fear factor helped me survive. His job was to book the shows, and my job was to wrestle and survive them.

Even though my good friend Bruno Sammartino was no longer the WWWF world champion, I still kept very busy from 1971 to 1973. During the summer of 1971, I decided to take some time off from the WWWF by choice. I had gotten some pretty anemic paychecks from Mr. McMahon and I had no real bargaining leverage.

Leverage was a concept that I'd been forced to grasp a handful of years earlier. I was teaching, coaching, and serving as a driver's education instructor in the summer, in addition to wrestling a full schedule. I had moved from the junior high to the high school, where I was a physical education teacher as well as an assistant varsity football coach.

In the spring of 1964, I received what I still refer to as "toilet education," and it did not have anything to do with my wife and I weaning the kids off diapers and onto porcelain. I was at a wrestling show in Lansing, Michigan, and I was sitting on the toilet when Bert Ruby and Leaping Larry Chene began arguing about money. When I heard Bert mention my name, I lifted my feet so they would not know I was listening. Bert said that he was going to cut my money in half and split it between Larry and Lou Klein.

The next night, I confronted Bert. He told me that I would not get as much money as the others because I was a teacher and had another paycheck coming in. I was ticked; I was their hottest heel and was working main events every night. It was not fair, and I told him so.

He did not book me for the next two weeks. He told me I had no bargaining power or leverage, and if I wanted to work, I should keep quiet. He told me that I should learn from the situation and I certainly did. From then on, I always made sure I had leverage.

That's when I decided to leave the WWWF and went to work with Bruno Sammartino. I loved working weekends in Pittsburgh, plus I worked for the Sheik during the week. It was a pretty sweet deal. I even went to Japan for three weeks that summer.

My first trip to Japan came in 1974 and we got the V.I.P. treatment. It was first class all the way—mints on the hotel pillows at night and all the sushi we could eat. I was there with other wrestlers including Jack Brisco, Victor Rivera, and Dick Garza, who was known as Mighty Igor.

We arrived in Tokyo and there was a press conference at the airport. Promoters, owners, and wrestlers Antonio Inoki and Giant Baba, who were huge stars in Japan, were paying for the trip. (They later turned on each other and had separate promotions.)

We were treated tremendously well during the entire trip. I forget how many guys were in our entourage, but one day they took us out for an afternoon of eating Kobe beef. We ate and ate and ate and it was fantastic—not exactly the drive-thru line at McDonalds, where we were limited to the dollar menu.

I was in Japan for around three weeks, but we really did not wrestle that much. It was a tour for Japanese television more than anything else. One day all of the wrestlers went to a water park. Another day, they took us shopping for pearls, watches, and things like that. Tailors came and measured us for custom suits that cost about one-third what they would've cost back home. There were also custom-made wrestling boots. Another day they took us to a spa and each wrestler had a geisha assigned to him. Even though we were all nude, there was no hanky panky going on. I swear on a stack of fortune cookies, Pat.

What wrestling we did was easy and very well done. Pro wrestling was huge in Japan. I loved the Japanese people. Even if they did not like you, they respected you. They did not boo, they hissed. Believe me, I heard a lot of hissing during those three weeks. It was like a giant car tire that had developed a leak.

I had a lot of fun with the people there. I remember going into a barber shop as a joke and told the barbers I wanted to have my hair cut. Remember, a Georgia peach sported an Afro compared to my head. The language barrier made it even funnier. They thought I wanted a shave. Finally, one of the barbers who spoke some English explained to me that I did not have any hair. I pulled my shirt down to prove otherwise. It was hilarious.

I experienced a different sort of hilarity on my second trip to Japan two years later. By this time, the Giant Baba and Inoki had split, and we were working for the Giant Baba. It was on this trip when I first met Bobby Backlund, who was then a raw rookie years away from becoming the WWF champ.

Working for the Giant Baba at the time was a masked wrestler called the Destroyer. He was an American, Dick Beyer, who had actually played football at Syracuse University and had graduated with a masters degree in education. In early 1963 he wrestled three sold-out matches against the Giant Baba in Los Angeles, and that is how their relationship began. Ten years later, starting in 1973, he wrestled in Japan for six straight years. He was a great help to all of us when we went to Japan to work.

Another one of my favorite guys on that trip was Danny Hodge, a talented amateur wrestler who had won three NCAA wrestling championships at the University of Oklahoma. While at Oklahoma, he went 46–0 with 36 pins. Danny could crush an apple in one hand. Honest to applesauce, he could turn a McIntosh into scrumptious apple cider with just a squeeze. He could also break a pair of pliers by just squeezing the handles. I imagine the folks at Sears hated him because they had a lifetime guarantee on all of their Craftsman tools.

On my second trip to Japan, I decided to go shopping for things that Pat might have wanted for our house. I went inside one store and the guys there took a liking to me. That night, we went to a high-end restaurant, ate very well, and drank expensive Scotch. We drove to and from the restaurant in Cadillacs, speeding all over town. If anyone happened to be in their way, they just honked the horn. It was like rush hour in New York City or Los Angeles, only we were the only ones on the road in big American cars.

I noticed as we were eating that a few patrons pointed their pinky fingers at us. Every time we wrestled in a different city, someone else would meet me and take me out for a very good time. The finger-pointing continued.

Finally, I invited Backlund and Hodge along. When they saw who I was going out with, they refused the invitation. The finger-pointing was apparently an act of appeasement. The pointing was being done with pinky fingers that had all been chopped off at the first joint. I had been hanging with the yakuza, the Japanese version of the mafia. I had been befriended by Don Corleone-san. But hey, at least I never had problems getting a table at good restaurants.

The way I figured it, I was two-for-two on my trips to Japan. I'd had wonderful times and unforgettable moments and I was looking forward to returning when I was asked back in 1979. But this time, things had definitely changed. Inoki was in charge of the promotion and suddenly the foreigners, or *gaijin*, were second-class citizens. The limousines were for the Japanese wrestlers, and we were transported in a rickety old bus. A rickshaw with a Suzuki motor would've been an improvement.

We were strictly blue-collar laborers in their eyes, and we were treated accordingly. Rented mules and migrant workers had more perks than we did. We wrestled twice a day and there were not many days off. I was not a happy camper—and believe me, when I am not happy, things do not go well for my employers. I refused to bow to their demands. Before every match a lady in a kimono would hand us flowers. We were supposed to hand them to the most beautiful young woman in the audience. Instead, I made sure I found her complete opposite. This infuriated the promoters but I did not care. I kept doing it again and again. Take that, FTD. You, too, Inoki.

Another wrestler on that tour was Bad, Bad Leroy Brown, whose ring name came from that Jim Croce song. His real name was Roland Daniels, and he stood maybe 6'3" and weighed more than 300 pounds. In Japan, they talked him into getting hit in the head with a beer bottle during one of the bouts. Roland asked me about it, and I told him that I had heard if you freeze the bottle and then put hot water in it, it would be easy to break.

But the Japanese promoters screwed it up. They used one of their big beer bottles. I don't think they froze it, either. They had to hit Roland in the head four times before it broke. He was already staggering after the first attempt. The only thing holding Roland up were the ropes, but they just kept hitting him. It was inhumane. I swear they nearly killed the kid in the ring. The next day, we were on the same old rickety bus when the limo carrying the Japanese wrestlers crept up alongside us. It pulled over and all the wrestlers were invited off the bus except me. By this time, they did not like me at all. Roland got off the bus, but very quickly got back on. Apparently, all the Japanese wrestlers were watching a tape of the previous night's match and kept rewinding it to the part where he was getting smashed in the head. They were laughing and laughing.

I knew then that I would never go back to wrestle in Japan. Roland Daniels died in 1988. They said he had a stroke.

In the spring of 1975, after my first trip to Japan, I got a call from Mr. McMahon. He said he had some dates for me. I thought maybe I had finally gained some leverage. Back then, the WWWF did television shows every three weeks, on Tuesdays and Wednesdays. That was perfect for me, since I could get two days' worth of television exposure and be back in school on Thursday. I went from wrestling tights to a school-teacher's duds. It was like Superman yanking off the cape and suit and pulling on Clark Kent's khakis.

Our three hours on Tuesdays were at the Philadelphia Arena. We would stay in a hotel in Reading and do another three hours in Hamburg. Afterward, we would join Mr. McMahon for a late dinner and a drink. Better make that plural. *Drinks* is a much more accurate word, and not even Carrie Nation riding shotgun with Elliot Ness could have stopped our imbibing.

One night I was sitting across from Mr. McMahon. He was three or four drinks into the night and his glasses were so far down the end of his nose that he looked like a much more slender St. Nick, minus the bag of presents. Staring directly at me, he announced that he respected a wrestler who spoke his mind when he believed he hadn't been paid enough. He then proclaimed that he always made things right.

It was time to find out if Mr. McMahon was truly St. Nick, or just a Scrooge who'd downed several martinis. I told him that when a wrestler worked hard and sold tickets, the promoter knew that better than anyone else. Why, I asked, should a wrestler come begging for what he has earned? With that, Mr. McMahon sat back in his chair and was silent. While he did not order an egg nog and break out into a hearty chorus of "Jolly Ol' St. Nicholas," I assumed I had made my point.

I knew for sure that I had made my point when, incredibly, I turned the toilet into an eavesdropping device once again some years later. I was sitting on the throne in Hamburg, Pennsylvania, and I heard voices talking about yours truly. Once again I lifted my feet and tried my darnedest to make sure there were no Enola Gay bombs dropping because I did not want Mr. McMahon and his son, Vince, to know that I was listening to them.

Mr. McMahon was explaining to Vince why George "the Animal" Steele was so valuable. Wow, what a front-row porcelain seat I had! Mr. McMahon said that they only needed me to fly in for two TV shoots, which equaled six televised shows. He went on to explain that I would be available for two months and they would do great business during those summer months. Then I would be gone, back to teaching and coaching, and that meant they did have to keep me around on the heavy end of the payroll.

That schedule served two important functions. Most of the other top heels spent weeks getting beat up while finishing their run, working one town at a time. Me, I was working all the main events at the same time and then went back to school. Sure, I made some good money, but I also saved Mr. McMahon and Vince a lot of money.

While I was known as the Animal, there came a time when I was asked to wrestle a *real* four-legged creature. In 1971, Newton Tattrie asked me to wrestle Victor the Bear. It was ratings week for the *Studio Wrestling* show, and Newton thought it would be great to advertise the upcoming match.

I told him there was no way I was wrestling Victor the Bear. I was not going to wrestle Yogi Bear, Boo Boo, or all of the Care Bears in a tag team bout. I was not afraid of Victor the Bear; I just thought it would be a poor business decision on my part. What kind of leverage would I gain from taking on not-so-gentle Ben? That was a carnival stunt, and not to be demeaning to carnies, but I did not think that was a promising path for job advancement. What would be next, arm wrestling a sloth?

Newton was a good guy. He tried to talk me into it by telling me that the bear was trained, declawed, and would be wearing a muzzle. He did everything but claim Victor was really a midget in a bear suit, but I still said no.

He obviously was not listening. Newton went ahead and advertised a Victor the Bear versus George "the Animal" Steele televised match. They plugged it all week, and the more it was plugged, the madder I got. I really believed wrestling a bear was an insult to the wrestling profession and me.

But there was the Victor the Bear's truck in the parking lot when the taxi dropped me off at Channel 11 the following weekend. I walked in and told Newton yet again that I would not wrestle the bear. He begged, and told me that if I did not wrestle Victor, he could lose everything.

We argued for a while. I told him he could take Victor to Jellystone Park and they could swipe picnic baskets. Or he could rent him out to Disney and have him join the Country Bear Jamboree. Or he could turn him into a bearskin rug and sell him to the good folks from PETA. Finally, Newton begged me to go in the ring and do my stuff and then David, who was Victor's trainer, would work the match.

Animal

When the time came for me to hit the ring, I launched right into my wild animal antics. I snorted and I stomped and it became so convincing that I almost wanted to shoot myself with a tranquilizer dart. Victor immediately became a little unnerved. He'd been trained to wrestle humans, not some sub-species like George "the Animal" Steele. Victor had a chain attached to his collar and I jerked it once or twice. I do not know if Victor got excited or nervous, but he started to go to the bathroom all over the ring. It was like he was overdosing on laxatives. Excrement was all over the ring, and if there had been a fan, it would've hit that, too. I shouted to announcer Bill Cardille, "Look at that. I scared the shit out of Victor!"

This was live television. Shortly after that night, Newton sold the Pittsburgh wrestling promotion to the Jacobs brothers of Buffalo, New York.

I am not sure Victor the Bear was much larger than Haystacks Calhoun, a great attraction in those days. Haystacks was listed at 607 pounds, and while I never knew his exact weight, he certainly did not do his shopping at Abercrombie & Fitch or his eating at a salad bar.

I spent a few weeks with Haystacks in Newfoundland. We shared a one-room apartment and believe me, there was not a whole lot of elbow room left when we both were home. Can you imagine the looks we got at the grocery store? People rushed in sheer panic to grab their eggs, milk, and Shredded Wheat before Haystacks started his grazing in earnest. He was really passionate about his food. We decided to split the grocery bill—which was a bum deal for me since mine was a Lilliputian by comparison—but I did not squawk.

After a wrestling show, I would go out and party. Haystacks would head back to our apartment, read the Bible, and then go to bed. The first night after a show I got back around 1:00 in the morning. Hungry, I opened the door slowly so I would not disturb Haystacks. As soon as the light in the refrigerator went on, he would start to sit up. I closed the door

84

slowly and he lay back down. Every time I opened the door, Haystacks would start to get up. Every time I closed it, he would lay back down. It was the craziest thing I had ever seen. I felt like Pavlov working with his dogs.

Haystacks was a great guy. I had only seen him get really mad one time. He ordered a BLT in a restaurant in Newfoundland and when he took his first bite, he got this funny look on his face. He called the waitress over and told her that there was no bacon on his sandwich. She replied that bacon was not included on a BLT. Haystacks exploded and screamed; "What is the B for?" The waitress answered, "Bread." I almost wet myself from laughing, and that made Haystacks even madder.

It was only about a year later when Haystacks had part of his leg amputated. Shortly after that, he died. Haystacks Calhoun read scripture every night and he was right with the Lord. I hope there's an all-you-can eat buffet for him in heaven.

If there is a dress code in heaven, I am not sure purple pantsuits are allowed. Back in the early 1970s, I was wrestling a television match in the old Philadelphia Arena and pantsuits were definitely in vogue. Sitting ringside was a very large and well-dressed African American woman. She was wearing a purple metallic pantsuit. Not only was her outfit loud, so was she. She kept shouting all kinds of vile things my way. She questioned my ancestry, my mother's ancestry, and did not inquire in PG-rated fashion, either. Finally, I'd had enough. I stepped halfway through the ropes and yelled "You!" I pointed her way and suddenly, the crotch area of her purple pantsuit turned a decidedly deeper shade of purple. How can I put this politely? I guess I cannot. The lady had pissed herself. Since I was on camera, I had to think fast. I did not want to lose my menacing presence by breaking out in laughter in the middle of a match. So I did what the Animal always did—I proceeded to put my face in a turnbuckle pad and started munching away. It was the only way I could think of to hide my face. I was laughing so hard I nearly cried.

Munching those high-fiber turnbuckles was the subject of my first real conversation with Rowdy Roddy Piper, a guy who I will always have a soft spot for. The first night we met, Hot Rod asked if he could ride with me. He said he wanted to talk and that he'd buy the beer. Rather than the traditional six-pack, he came out of the store carrying a case. Piper would finish a beer and toss the empty bottle into the backseat. Since I was driving a rental, I did not have a problem with it. About four beers into the night, Piper said he had a real problem with me and the way I worked. He said that I was exposing the wrestling business. Now, I am not the smartest guy in the world and I never appeared on *Jeopardy!*, but I still did not have a clue what Piper was talking about. He said that when I tore into a turnbuckle pad and threw the stuffing all over the ring, people could see how soft the padding was. He said that when a wrestler rammed another wrestler's noggin into the padding fans would know that it did not hurt. I told him that everyone who comes to a wrestling match can see the padding, and that I never rammed an opponent's head into the padded turnbuckle. Instead, I aimed for the steel post and advised him to do likewise. He told me that he saw my point and that was the end of that particular conversation. I shook my head a few times as I drove the car. Maybe it is no surprise that no wrestler has ever split the atom.

Back then, the WWF paid for our rental cars. We checked into a motel and Piper asked if he could have the keys. Fifteen minutes later, he was back at the hotel. He'd been in an accident. Three other Lincoln Town Cars were wrecked that same night. The policy of the office paying for our rentals came to a crashing halt.

I liked Roddy Piper; he was just in a different zip code some of the time. But who wasn't, especially in our line of work? Still, he always seemed to have a chip on his shoulder. One night he inadvertently did the Frankenstein's monster routine. He reached for a towel and accidentally stuck his finger in an empty light socket. While he did not wind up with bolts in his head, he was in pretty bad shape. We went to Milwaukee for a show the following night, and I sent out for a massage therapist, hoping that she could help him. I guess it was not much of a shock that she didn't offer much relief. Following that show, I dropped him off at O'Hare in Chicago so he could fly home.

I would soon really be flying high in the WWF, and it had to do with one of the most remarkable transformations this side of Dr. Frankenstein's monster. That was the moment I went into the ring as one of the wildest, most hated heels in the history of professional wrestling and emerged from it as warm and fuzzy as a teddy bear.

It was a six-man tag team match. My team was made up of the hated George "the Animal" Steele, the vilified Iron Sheik, and the despised Nikolai Volkoff. Our opponents were the red, white, and blue American team of Ricky "the Dragon" Steamboat, Barry Windham, and Mike Rotundo.

I wound up getting pinned by Windham, and during the match the Iron Sheik and Volkoff refused to be tagged by me. After the bout I fought off an attack by the Iron Sheik and Volkoff. Shaken, I had to be consoled by Captain Lou Albano.

A few moments later, I was led from the ring by a sympathetic Captain Lou. Gene Okerlund was conducting an interview near the entranceway with Sheik and Volkoff, and I decided to throw a few punches at Volkoff before going backstage. It was all on *Saturday Night's Main Event*.

The crowd went wild. All of a sudden, I went from heel to hero; from bad guy to babyface. It was as if I had punched out a mugger trying to take Uncle Sam's wallet.

It truly was a magical moment, and that was when I decided to retire from teaching and coaching and become a full-time wrestler. I was 48 years old.

From then on, George "the Animal" Steele could do no wrong. My conduct in the ring did not change much. I would still beat up my opponents. I would rip at their arms and tie them up in my autographed flying hammerlock. I'd show my green tongue and eat turnbuckles. But instead of being repulsed, the fans ate it up. I would still chase referees and announcers, I would throw chairs. The fans loved it.

Then I would bring youngsters into the ring. I was a cartoon character and the kids embraced my persona. One of the youngsters would be the referee and lift my hand in victory. Another would be the announcer and shout over the microphone that George "the Animal" Steele was the winner. I would dance around the ring like I was John Travolta in *Saturday Night Fever*, only my white suit would've been XXXL.

I was working with Adrian Adonis, who was coming back on the next show with Hulk Hogan. The office wanted to get Adrian over strong but did not want to hurt my momentum. Adrian came up with a great idea. I was all over him until he rolled out of the ring and got a Miss Elizabeth poster. He brought that poster into the ring and slowly tore it up. I acted as though he was ripping my heart to pieces. When he threw the scraps to the ground, I dropped to my knees. I picked up each piece gently and began putting them together like a puzzle. While I was obsessed with making Miss Elizabeth whole again, Adrian went to the top rope and dropped a knee on the back of my head, leading to a pin.

Undaunted, I proceeded to roll over and continued to put the Miss Elizabeth jigsaw puzzle back together again. The fans at the Philadelphia Spectrum went silent. When they realized what was happening, they blew the roof off the place. The pin was not important to the Animal, but Miss Elizabeth was.

CHAPTER 8

A Hunted Animal

Clark Kent was the mild-mannered one. Superman was the guy who favored blue tights and a red cape. He had a mean streak, too. Especially if your name was Lex Luthor or your rock collection leaned toward kryptonite. They were one in the same, Clark and Superman. Sort of like Sybil, only with a jock strap and Aqua Velva.

Pop culture is peppered with split personalities. Dr. Jekyll and Mr. Hyde. Dr. Bruce Banner and the Incredible Hulk. Jim Myers and George "the Animal" Steele.

I did a good George "the Animal" Steele. So good that it was sometimes frightening to the fans—even to myself.

This was a night that the drooling, maniacal George "the Animal" Steele took total control of the body that we shared like a two-bedroom apartment.

Truth be told, we almost got our butt kicked that night in New York City. Or would that be butts?

I had already fought Bruno Sammartino, the WWWF champion, once that year. They tried to stop the match because I had a few drops of blood on my bald but thoroughly beautiful head. I was in the middle of whaling on Bruno when the referee chose to stop the match. I was screaming at the referee. I was critiquing his performance. It was not a PG-13 rating, either.

"You Italian referees are always protecting your champion!" I screamed.

All right, the words between those quotation marks might have been cleansed in Clorox for this book. Obviously I was no diplomat.

Now, Bruno and I were going at it again in front of a sold-out crowd at Madison Square Garden. I went in for the kill. As I attacked Bruno with my foreign object, he caught me in the midsection with a stiff boot and my taped weapon went flying. The referee saw that I was in trouble so he waved for the match to continue.

That served to excite the largely Italian crowd even more. The fans were running up and down the aisles. I thought, *Wow, one of those jerks is going to fall out of the balcony tonight.*

They always went wild when Bruno was in control, but on this particular night at MSG, their excitement went to a whole new level. The great fans in the Big Apple were really getting their money's worth. Both Bruno and I were committed to it. Or should I have *been* committed?

The way things transpired that night, I really was not too sure. There was an 11:00 PM curfew. It was 10:15 and the fans had just popped like they never had before. The problem was, we had 45 minutes to go.

So, I cut off Bruno's assault with a crotch shot. Pro wrestling is a tough business. There are no niceties involved in an assault on a man's crotch. Just ask John Bobbitt. I proceeded to put my boots to the fallen champion and the crowd went crazy. You would have thought I'd put the Pope in a headlock or sent the Flying Nun hurtling out of the ring.

Every fan in the Garden saw it when I got my foreign object back from Bruno. That is, everyone but the referee. He must have been from the Stevie Wonder School of Officiating. Helen Keller must have been his prom date. People were really screaming now. Enraged spectators were rushing toward the ring screeching to the befuddled referee that I had regained my weapon.

It's probably time that I come clean about what my foreign object was all of those years. It was a bottle opener from Japan, a beer bottle opener. It spent its early life opening beverages like Kirin, Asahi, and Suntory. Through my persuasive negotiating skills, a bartender in the Land of the Rising Sun gave me the opener as a gift.

Then it went from opening bottles to opening cuts on the likes of Sammartino, Savage, and Hogan.

The first time I tried to use the literal foreign object, I taped the beer opener to my skin. As soon as the sweat started to flow, I had a problem. The opener slipped out of my tights, the referee spotted it, and I was disqualified. From that match on, I always reversed the tape so the sticky side was out. I never had the opener—or anything else—fall out of my trunks again.

The point of the foreign object was to put the heat on the referee. It added to crowd participation, which usually meant crowd irritation. I always told the referee to disqualify me if he ever saw me using my foreign object. I promptly made sure everyone in the arena, including the guy sitting in the cheap seats who needed a Hubble telescope to see the action, saw me cheat with my foreign object. Everyone but the referee, that is.

That would infuriate the fans, who for the bulk of my career hated me with a passion usually reserved for cheating husbands or bill collectors.

They certainly hated me that night in New York City. Once again, I never even had to use the foreign object on Bruno Sammartino. All I needed was its menacing presence. Bruno and I were exchanging holds, and every time Bruno got the upper hand, I would simply reach for the foreign object again. Again and again and again.

The fans loved Bruno and hated the Animal.

It was about 10:45 PM when I went to my foreign object again. As I went for it, Bruno caught me with a shot to the jaw that Joe Frazier would have been proud to have autographed. He knocked me all over the ring. The fans went nuts. They were blowing the roof off the place.

Bruno continued to beat me. The more he beat me, the more the fans ate it up. Bruno had his adrenaline going and he threw me into the ropes with such force that I came launching off them like a rocket. I figured this was my chance. I would give Bruno a flying tackle and knock him on his rear end and regain control of the match. But he sidestepped me and caught me full force in the throat with my own foreign object. I landed on the back of my head and shoulders. I was dizzy. I was a beaten man, and the Italians were ready for a great victory.

There's a phrase you don't hear too often—Italians and great victory. It's 11:00: do you know where Mussolini's head is? But on this night in the Garden, they were all chanting as one. They wanted Bruno to win so badly they could taste it, Prego and all.

But I had other plans. I rolled out of the ring to recuperate. In those days, we were allowed a 20-count on the floor and a 10-count on the ring apron, and I used up pretty much every second of that time. I milked the clock like it had udders. It did not take the fans long to realize that I was stalling.

As the referee shoved Bruno back to a neutral corner, I came back in the ring. When he rushed toward me again, I dove back through the ropes to the safety of the floor. Yep, I was stalling again.

Seven minutes until curfew. I went through the ropes and rushed Bruno. I thought I might catch him off guard. It almost worked, but Bruno caught me with the quickest arm drag I had ever seen. I rushed him again, and he caught me with another arm drag. As he came up, I finally caught him with a single leg and he went down. He put his free leg on my chest and sent me hurtling back into the ropes. Again, I shot off them like a NASA product, but the champ flipped me and I was back on the floor.

I had shot my wad. I was exhausted. I looked at the clock and I could not believe it. There were still four minutes to go. I took a 19-count and rolled into the ring once again. Then I went back out of the ring. The fans were enraged. They were shouting the vilest things at me. They were throwing anything they could get their hands on.

I was a one-man leper colony. Even my manager, the Grand Wizard, moved as far away from me as possible. He still got drenched in beer. Finally, he scurried to the safety of the locker room.

Things were getting wild. I kept stalling, and that got the fans overheated. As the clock ticked away it became apparent that the Animal was going to rob their champion of his much-deserved victory. With the curfew looming, Sammartino clamped all of his 285 pounds down on me and thought he had me pinned, but I wriggled free and scrambled out to the ring apron. When I rolled back into the ring, my exit was quicker than a white-tail buck that mistakenly wanders into a National Rifle Association picnic. This time I went to the floor and the crowd of some 20,000 booed and jeered and questioned both my manhood and lineage.

Once back into the ring, Bruno and I locked up. We wrestled for another minute. Once again, he almost had me pinned. Once again, I spun away and headed for the apron. It might as well have been my mom's apron strings. The fans were livid.

The bell rang, the 11:00 PM curfew had arrived, and even the referee was disgusted when he had to raise both our hands in the middle of the ring. The match was a draw.

But Bruno was not ready to take out some crayons and draw pretty pictures. He had already cut me once during the match, and it looked like I'd been pouring V8 juice all over my head. Then, he wrested a folding chair out of my hands and proceeded to smack me in the head with it.

More blood splattered across the mat. This was not a sight for vegans or the weak-hearted.

Bruno jumped to the middle of the ring to pronounce himself champion. Everyone in the crowd agreed with his decision, judging by the deafening ovation.

Once again, I left the ring in the protection of the police. Officers in riot gear carrying night sticks surrounded me as we walked to the locker room.

That was hardly the first (or last) time I needed an escort out of the ring. Earlier in my career, I wrestled with Walter "Killer" Kowalski, who was from Windsor and had trained under Bert Ruby, too.

We worked as a tag team for a while. Our first match together was against Haystacks Calhoun and Victor Rivera. We were wrestling in Springfield, Massachusetts, which was one of the toughest towns in the country back then. It also had a large Hispanic population. Guess which team the fans were cheering for?

I had these very high boots on. It was tough to find a pair of laces that fit them properly, so I got these long laces and I was going to cut them after I had laced the boots up. As I was grabbing for a pair of scissors, Walter said, "Don't cut them. Don't ever waste anything, kid."

So, I listened to him and I did not cut the laces. I just tucked them into the boots. We got into the match and quickly discovered that Haystacks was big as a Peterbilt and Victor was pretty quick and agile.

In the midst of the match, Killer Kowalski told me to take my shoelace and tie it around Haystacks's neck. The referee was talking to me and did not know what I was doing, but the fans certainly did. They were getting really hot. All of a sudden here comes a countryman of Rivera's with a knife about as long as a machete. I saw him coming but I couldn't get away, because the shoelace is around Haystack's neck and it is also laced through my boot. We were bonded together like Siamese twins. I figured I was about to meet my maker, but I was not close to being ready. I did not even know the Lord's first name yet, much less the Lord's Prayer. The hereafter for me looked to be one where central air is a necessity.

Only rather than taking the machete to me, the guy simply reached into the ring and sliced the shoelace. I said a short prayer and the match went on.

Later on, the four of us were wrestling in Atlantic City. The arena was packed and I was beating on Victor and the fans were really getting hot. One of the fans picked up a steel folding chair and threw it at me. I ducked out of the way and it hit Victor and the blood started gushing. It was the Alamo once again and the odds were about the same. The fans stormed the ring. We were in the middle of a full-blown riot. Somehow we bobbed and weaved our way to the concession area. There were two metal doors, and the fans were intent on coming through them. We hid in a janitorial closet until the cops finally arrived, complete with dogs—and I'm not talking poodles or Yorkshire terriers. I'm talking German shepherds with bad attitudes and nasty growls. The crowd finally dispersed and we finally got to the locker room. This time it was Killer Kowalski's turn to be hot.

"You're going to get us killed!" he shouted.

Walter was right. The mentality in the ring is to get the crowd hot and then bring them down by letting your opponent start to get the upper hand. Then it's back to getting them hot again.

I learned my lesson...at least for a while. And then I faced Bruno Sammartino in Madison Square Garden.

When the match ended, a large contingent of New York City police officers rushed me to the locker room, where Blackjack Lanza was waiting. He looked me over, smirked, and shook his head. He noticed that my head looked like a Big Mac minus the lettuce and cheese. "Sounds like you got a lot of heat out there tonight, George," he said. "What is that, blood or ketchup?"

Truthfully, it was both.

Lanza and I planned a taxi to the airport. We were both flying Northwest; I was getting out in Detroit and he was heading home to Minneapolis. Both of us were happy to be spending the rest of the weekend with our families.

After I showered and changed, police officers and Madison Square Garden security people walked us to the regular exit. The door opened and we were confronted by a mob scene straight out of Mary Shelley's *Frankenstein*. The same angry looks. The same outraged screams. The same vows about killing the monster. Only this monster and I shared the same return address. About the only thing the mob lacked was torches.

"No way out here, guys," said one of the cops. "There's at least a thousand angry people waiting out there. In the rain."

Maybe that was why there were no torches.

We then made our way down to the Felt Forum, where the closed-circuit television system allowed the overflow crowd to watch the matches. The room, which could hold 4,000 people, had been ransacked. It looked like John Belushi's fraternity house. Or Charlie Sheen's hotel room. Furniture was overturned and thrown everywhere. Big-screen televisions had been smashed. Food scraps and wrappers were strewn about.

Another cop opened the outside door an inch. Another mob scene. Once again, everybody was extremely pissed and everyone was fuming about George "the Animal" Steele.

The security force guided us to the Eighth Avenue exit. Once again, the streets were filled with a roiling mob. Hundreds of wrestling fans, and all told, about 100 combined IQ points. They were not discussing Dickens or Keats. Their need was much more basic. How do you spell d-i-s-m-e-m-b-e-r-m-e-n-t?

Who said three-year-olds cannot be sharp-dressed young men? You can tell by my wide smile that I had not started school yet.

I was six when my mom and dad got me to sit still for a minute for this picture. Since I was in grade school, my smile was not quite as wide.

Notice that the pencil I'm holding as I sat at the desk in our living room is upside down. Nothing could be more symbolic of how I felt about school, due to my struggles with dyslexia.

It is fall in the early 1980s. I am coaching football at my alma mater, Madison High School, in suburban Detroit.

Don't be fooled: it was no pyramid scheme when we won the state wrestling championship in 1969 at Madison High School. It was done through good, honest hard work.

One of the real joys of coaching in high school was working with my younger brother, Jack, who is sitting to my left.

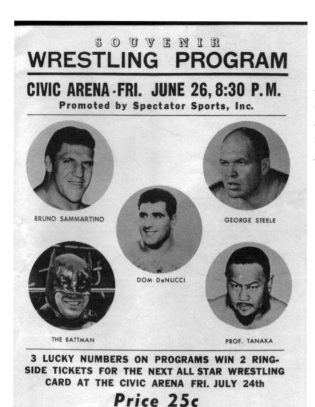

I still had a little
bit of hair left when
I was wrestling at
the Civic Arena in
Pittsburgh.

Although Bruno
Sammartino and
I had some vicious
matches in our time
in the ring, we were
actually very good
friends out of it.

It did not have to be Thanksgiving in George "the Animal" Steele's world to enjoy a little stuffing. (Photo courtesy of WWE)

After tearing into a turnbuckle, Randy Savage decided to tear into me during one of our many matches. We battled non-stop for nearly two years. (Photo courtesy of WWE)

I am flanked by school board president Al Morrison (left) and superintendent Randy Speck during the stadium dedication game at Madison High School.

It really meant a lot to me when they dedicated the football field at Madison High in my name.

"Unbelievable," said a cop. "Let's head for Penn Station."

That's where Lanza and I finally got into a cab. The ride did not last long. Very quickly, we were stopped by a throng of irate wrestling fans who had just come from behind the Garden.

"There he is! There he is! Let's get the SOB!" someone yelled.

I was that SOB. I don't mind telling you I was more than a little nervous. It was one thing to taunt fans from the ring; it was another when you're in a cab and they are staring at you through the glass like you're a puffer fish.

People pointed and shouted. The crowd began to surge toward us. A larger group heard the commotion and stepped around the corner in time to see us. The two groups merged. There was plenty of screaming and cursing.

We were on a one-way street, and stuck behind a truck at a stoplight. Very quickly, hundreds of less-then-adoring fans surrounded us. They began doing a Ringo Starr number on the cab, banging their fists against the vehicle, intent on revenge since I had ruined their hero's chance at victory. They began rocking the cab back and forth.

"Oh my God, we're going to get killed. Who are you guys anyway?" asked the terrified cabbie.

Knowing I had to do something to try to put an end to the ugly scene, I flung open the door to the cab, jumped out, shoved my hand into the pocket of my trousers, and acted as if I had a gun. "Get back! Get back! Get back all of you or I'll shoot!" I shouted.

Now, keep in mind this was years ago. It was before every Tom, Dick, and Harry was carrying an Uzi, a sawed-off shotgun, or some sort of weapon. The trick worked, but only on a very temporary basis. Within seconds, the mob realized I was unarmed and got even more riled up.

They began pelting the cab with trash. We were still stuck behind the truck, but the signal had finally changed to green.

"Go! Go! Go!" Lanza and I shouted.

Animal

Just then, the truck in front of us sputtered and stalled. The mob
cheered and surged toward us. The terrified cabbie fumbled with the
door handle, trying to get away. Lanza and I yelled at him to stay
inside, but he continued to fumble with the handle. I punched a hole
through the cab's plastic barrier between the front and back seats,
grabbed him around the neck, and told him that if he left we would
be dead meat.

Chances were increasing that we would all be roadkill anyway.

The mob was back on the cab again. The people were absolutely going
berserk. They were out of their minds. They were wild-eyed. They were
maniacal. Once again, the mob began to shake the cab. The tires on one
side easily lifted off the asphalt, first one way and then the next. I was
sure we'd tip over in a few seconds.

"Drive under the truck!" Lanza screamed at the cabbie. "Ram this
piece of junk under the truck's rear bumper!"

Panic-stricken, the driver gunned it and crashed into the truck,
ramming the hood under the bumper as people stumbled out of the way.
Metal grated as the hood crumbled and wedged beneath the bumper just
enough to keep us from being flipped over.

Lanza's quick thinking probably saved our lives, but we were still not
moving and worse, we were still surrounded by Bruno Sammartino's
livid fans.

People once again began hitting the cab with whatever they could
find and the back window shattered.

The traffic signal turned green and the stalled truck restarted its
engine and lumbered forward. A bizarre parade crept down West 33rd
Street: a smoke-belching truck straight out of an episode of *The Beverly
Hillbillies* followed by a battered taxicab driven by some poor, frightened
man followed by a screeching mob. Kennedy Airport, while only 18 miles
from midtown Manhattan, might as well have been three continents
away.

98

We relaxed a little when the driver turned onto 8th Avenue and no one had banged on our windows for half a block. We were finally heading toward the relative safety of the airport.

However, as we approached West 34th Street, we saw that the usual heavy Saturday night crosstown traffic congested the street. Incredibly, half a dozen fanatics caught up with us and jogged alongside, pounding on the fenders and roof with every step and demanding that I be turned over to the pack for disposal.

"Where's the cops?" our nervous driver muttered. "They're never around when you want and in your face when you don't." He leaned on the horn and tried to weave around as many vehicles as possible.

We had almost reached West 35th Street when I glanced out the broken rear window. The shocking scene behind us was something right out of an old Hollywood movie. I nudged Lanza to take a look. It seemed as though the entire mob was plowing its way through the bumper-to-bumper traffic like a gang of pirates swarming over a ship, running around trucks and cars and sliding over the hoods to reach us.

You had to hand it to Bruno's fans. What they lacked in smarts they more than made up for in stamina. Too bad the bout with Sammartino hadn't take place much more recently like, say, a month or so ago. We have gotten so fat and out of shape in this country, we look like manatees in sweatpants, Bruno's fans would not have lasted more than a block and a half.

Lanza stared out the window, groaned, then pounded on what was left of the plastic barrier separating the seats. "Move this thing any way you can, driver. They're still coming."

We were chased like that for four long, traffic-snarled blocks, narrowly escaping disaster each time.

"Look at what's happened to my cab," the driver shouted over his shoulder. "It's your fault that it's a wreck."

"We did not do anything except try to save our own butts—and yours, too," I replied. "Just keep driving so we can make our flight. We'll take care of everything."

Upset, the cab driver grumbled about the damage to his vehicle all the way to Kennedy. When we finally reached the airport, Lanza and I each tossed him a very generous $10 tip, hurried to the gate, and barely made our flight.

During the flight home, I recalled a conversation I'd recently had with someone who had tried to tell me that professional wrestling was only entertainment, as scripted as one of Spielberg's flicks, and as fraudulent as a politician's smile.

What a waste of time that talk had been. I knew the truth and had the scars to prove him wrong. Devoted fans of the sport had made it abundantly clear, again and again, that wrestling was a deadly serious business, both in and out of the ring.

On the flight home, I also reflected on why I had gotten involved in professional wrestling, how my life had been split into two different worlds, and how I was struggling to survive them both.

Needless to say, the return match sold out the following month. While it was Jim Myers who flew into Kennedy from Detroit that day, it was George "the Animal" Steele who stepped into the ring to take on Bruno Sammartino that night.

Sybil wore a jockstrap. Clark Kent had back hair. It was time for the high school teacher and coach from Michigan to be vilified by thousands in the Big Apple once again.

It was just a month after our wild night in the cab, and if Mr. McMahon had had his way, it would have been a cage match between Bruno Sammartino and George "the Animal" Steele. There was a slight problem: the New York State Athletic Commission gave the idea a thumbs down. They did not think the Animal should be caged.

Mr. McMahon and I were very disappointed. I really wanted that match. It was getting late into the summer and it was nearly time for me to pack away my wrestling gear and hang a whistle around my neck for the next nine months. George was going to be put away in a box and Jim was going to checking in at school soon. I figured a cage match was one way to put Bruno over in a spectacular way.

So, I suggested a money cage match instead. While there wouldn't be any bars, the risk of losing money would be a mighty strong reason to stay in the ring. It was decided that it would cost either wrestler $500 if they went to the ring apron, and $1,000 if they went to the MSG floor.

Once again, the fans loved Bruno and despised me. Someone with thinner skin might have been offended, but that was never an affliction that bothered me. I basked in hatred and bathed in infuriation. That, plus a little bubble bath once in a while.

Bruno and I had another wild brawl. Every time I'd roll out of the ring, the fans began a thunderous monetary countdown. The champion always won in a cage match, and the end result of this contest was no different. We gave them their money's worth.

Jim Myers was going home to coach his football team again. The assistant coaches had done the dirty work in the weight room and in conditioning. Practice was officially beginning, and the head coach would join his staff and his players.

Soon, the kids in gym class would soon be standing at the ready. They'd have on the T-shirts and the shorts that Coach Myers demanded.

Good-bye, Madison Square Garden. Hello, Madison Heights and Madison High School. Mr. Split Personality had a split in his head that was still seeping blood.

Fortunately, Pat and the kids were getting used to seeing Dad come home in that kind of shape. So were the kids who populated the huddle every fall.

CHAPTER 9

There Was Nothing Biblical About These Ribs

God made Eve from one of Adam's ribs. God did not slather Eve with any barbecue sauce. If He did, it was not in the Bible. When they bit into that apple in the Garden of Eden, the McIntosh was not yanked from the mouth of a pig.

No, the ribs you are about to devour were practical jokes perpetrated on one wrestler or another. Verily, it is so. Thou Shalt Not Rib is not a commandment.

One of the recurrent ribs was referred to as Mabel. Although it was never pulled on me, I remember sitting in a dressing room in Jackson, Michigan, with Leaping Larry Chene and Lou Klein, and they kept repeating, "Mabel is coming tonight." I had to ask them what they were talking about.

There was a new fellow with us. His name was Klondike Bill and he was up from Georgia by way of Canada, I think. He was a very nice guy, a real friendly sort. He was also a pretty big guy, about 6'0" and 370 pounds. He had dark, shaggy hair and a beard that Grizzly Adams would've been proud to own. He wore blue jeans with a white rope as a belt in the ring.

After the show, we all drove the 90 minutes or so back to Detroit on eastbound I-94 and went directly to the Eddystone Hotel on Cass Avenue, where we all had a couple of drinks at the bar.

While we were sitting there, this pretty enough gal who was a little on the five-and-dime side started coming on to Klondike Bill. The Eddystone was frequented by a lot of hookers, so that sort of behavior was not exactly out of the ordinary. Those kinds of working girls are not paid for taking dictation, fetching coffee, or teaching proper diction. But the women hardly ever bothered the wrestlers. They were not interested in the Wonder Bread and bologna crowd, I guess.

This one gal ended up taking Klondike Bill home with her. After they had been gone 15 or 20 minutes, Larry Chene and Lou Klein jumped up and said, "Come on, time to go. Time to go!"

All the wrestlers rushed out the door and I followed along. This gal lived maybe a mile away from the Eddystone. When we got there, we piled out of the cars and hid behind trees and bushes and other cars parked on the street. While the name of the rib was Mabel, this gal's name was Dorothy.

She took Klondike Bill into her place and pretty quickly told him she had to slip into something more comfortable. When Klondike Bill heard that, his reaction was Pavlovian, slobber and all. He started to take off his shoes, socks, shirt, and pants.

Suddenly, this big truck driver came bursting through the front door of Dorothy's house. He screamed, "What the heck is going on? I knew that she was cheating on me!" He pulled a gun, raced past Klondike Bill, and headed straight into the back of the house, where Dorothy had gone. *Bang! Bang!* Terrified, Klondike Bill grabbed his clothes and raced out of the house, going nearly 100 miles per hour. All of us were laughing so hard we were nearly crying.

When he got out into the street, he saw all of us and knew he'd been had. I am surprised he did not have a heart attack.

Klondike Bill was a really good guy, just a little on the gullible side. He was the target of a couple more ribs. Another time, we went to a place in Detroit called the Gold Dollar. It featured a show of female impersonators. For the uninformed, those are men who look like women while retaining the male plumbing. There were some really beautiful female impersonators and Terry was the star of the show. Or was it Terri?

Anyway, Terry came over and spent some time with Klondike Bill. Terry was absolutely gorgeous—until you realized that he wore a jockstrap instead of panties. There were signs in the Gold Dollar informing patrons that the "ladies" were female impersonators, but Klondike Bill did not seem to get it. About a week later, we all went in again with a new guy, and Terry came over and said we had better smarten Klondike Bill up—he had been in there every night for a week!

That's when we told Bill that Terry was not a beautiful woman. He did not wear Chanel No. 5, he favored Old Spice. When he shaved, it was not his legs, it was his mug.

There was a third rib involving Klondike Bill. Just around the corner from the Eddystone was another hotel, where the midget wrestlers stayed. That's quite a visual, isn't it? The midgets preferred to be called "midgets," by the way. They were not "little people" or whatever is politically correct these days. In wrestling, they were midgets. In contrast, Klondike Bill was a massive man. While he never really made it to wrestling's big time, he was a lot of fun to be around.

Promoter Jack Britton usually had six or eight midgets working. They would go all over the world to wrestle and were very popular. Some of the midgets had just come back from Montreal, and while they were in the city in Quebec, they claimed a beautiful girl had seen them wrestle and had come back to Detroit with them. All she wanted to do is make love, they said.

According to the midgets, this gal didn't discriminate based on height. She liked big men, too, and few were bigger than Klondike Bill. They kept talking about how beautiful she was and how insatiable she was and how much she wanted Bill. They talked about it so long that I was worried we might need a tranquilizer gun, a whip, and a chair to keep Bill away from their hotel room.

We had all been at another wrestling show in Jackson, and the midgets kept the talk up all the way back to Detroit. We got back to the Eddystone and they told Klondike Bill she was waiting for him in their room. After a couple of drinks, we all said good night, but instead of going home we raced across the street and hid in the midgets' hotel room. That was no easy feat. I mean, there must've been 12 full-size wrestlers inside the room and not one of us could be called petite. We were behind couches, under beds, crouching behind doors, and staying hidden pretty much anywhere you could jam 300-plus pounds of flesh.

One of the midgets arrived at the door with Bill and said he'd go in to see if the girl was ready for him. Instead, there was an inflatable doll in the bed. The setup was perfect. Moments later, Bill raced into the room. There he was, standing naked as Michelangelo's David, with 12 wrestlers coming out from their hiding places, laughing uproariously.

I know these ribs sound juvenile, but we were all just a bunch of big kids. All right, a bunch of XXXL kids.

Not all of us were XXXL, of course. People loved the midgets, and that included wrestling fans, wrestlers, and a lot of women. They were so cute and cuddly, and in the ring they always wrestled tag team bouts that were full of action. They were just great entertainers. On the other hand, cute and cuddly might not be the way you would describe trolls. Did you ever read much by way of Aesop or Grimm? Midgets and dwarves hung out with the likes of Snow White. Trolls had warts with hair growing out of them, bad teeth, and even worse dispositions. They were like Ewoks with lower intestinal problems.

Fuzzy Cupid, one of the midget wrestlers, was a friend of mine. He was one midget who looked like a troll. His real name was Leon Stap. His parents were of normal stature, but when he was seven years old, Fuzzy suffered from infantile paralysis and spent six years in the hospital.

Fuzzy saw his first wrestling match in Galveston, Texas, where he met promoter Norman Brown, who sent him to Detroit for training. Cupid had his pro wrestling debut in 1952.

Once, Fuzzy and I were headed to a show in Wisconsin. We were driving through Chicago and we were hungry, so we stopped at one of those restaurants built on top of the freeway overpasses.

We were up toward the front of the restaurant waiting for a table when I noticed they had this big display of troll dolls for sale. I asked the girl behind the counter if she had a patent for those dolls. She said, "I don't know what you mean." I asked her again if she had a patent, and she just looked at me quizzically. That's when Fuzzy Cupid jumped out from behind me and growled, "That's me! Those are my dolls!" The poor girl just jumped up in shock and ran away from the register. A little bit later, Fuzzy and I were sitting at a booth eating some burgers and fries. The same girl walked past and did not see Fuzzy. He growled at her, "You again!" and she ran off screaming.

Midgets always seemed to date tall women. I don't know what that was all about, and I never really asked any of the women you would constantly see towering over their dates. But I did ask Fuzzy Cupid once, and he explained it very succinctly. Before you read on, beware: this is not the sort of explanation that you'd hear in pew number four on Sunday morning at church, or one that would get the *Good Housekeeping*

Seal of Approval. But since I am going to tell it, I just hope God grades on a curve.

Fuzzy Cupid explained the attraction this way: "When we're toe to toe, our nose is in it. When we're lips to lips, our toes are in it."

Geez, how romantic. Is that a white dove I just saw fly by? I swear that was Cupid pulling back on a bow, ready to let an arrow go.

Unfortunately for the midgets, things did not stay all hugs and kisses. Political correctness did them in. Eventually, midgets were no longer midgets. They were little people, and that did not have the same sizzle on the marquee, I guess. They began to outfit themselves in Velcro coats and pants and bars used them as human darts in dwarf-tossing competitions. I would not exactly call that progress, would you? One giant leap for mankind, one very small step for little people. Sorry, Neil Armstrong.

When I first started wrestling, Bert Ruby thought it would be best if I had a manager. His name was Louie Papineau and everybody loved him. Louie was Canadian and had been quite a hockey player in his day. He even tried out for the Windsor Spitfires. He never drank or smoked; he was just a quality person.

We were doing a show in Detroit one night. Louie had only been my manager for six or eight weeks. He had a bout against Gino Brito, and then when he got back into the locker room, he collapsed and died. The autopsy later said he suffered a cerebral hemorrhage, and apparently he had been in a car accident a month earlier and had complained of neck pain.

Johnny Gates was on that same card. He was a guy who had absolutely never won a wrestling match. He would go into the ring and let everyone, including the midgets, beat him up. Johnny, along with all of the rest of us, were in the locker room when Louie dropped dead. After Johnny got over his momentary shock, he suggested we carry

Louie back into the ring while the body was still warm. "I can finally get a win," he said.

Gallows humor to be sure, but there was a lot of that in wrestling.

Another particular rib occurred years later, after the WWF had exploded in popularity. We had a show in a town down south, and Lex Luger was being set up by Owen Hart. Owen was a member of the famous Hart wrestling family and he was another Canadian, born in Calgary, Alberta. Owen was the youngest of 12 children born to Stampede Wrestling promoter and Hall of Famer Stu Hart and his wife, Helen.

Lex was driving, Owen was in the back seat, and Davey Boy Smith was riding shotgun. Davey Boy and Owen were pals. Davey Boy was from England, but he had relocated to Canada to train under Owen's dad. In fact, he married the Hart's youngest daughter, Diana.

Lex was always a fast driver, particularly when he was leaving a show. Fans always milled around wanting autographs and Lex would take off as quickly as he could. Maybe two blocks from the arena, a siren started to wail and police lights flashed in the rearview mirror. Lex immediately turned a little pale. He did not want another speeding ticket.

The officer walked up to the car and leaned into the driver's side window.

"Is there a fire?" he asked in a heavy drawl. This officer was right out of *Smokey and the Bandit*, trooper hat and all.

Lex explained that we were wrestlers and were just trying to escape from the big crowd at the arena.

From the seat next to Lex, Davey Boy told the cop to shut the hell up.

The officer asked, "What did he say?"

Then Owen Hart shouted, "Come on, we have to go!"

The officer asked again, "What did he say?"

Lex tried to explain that nobody had said anything, and that is when the officer told him to shut up, that he was responsible for everybody in that car and he was about a half-inch away from being arrested.

Lex started to get irritated at that point. He began to sputter and was just about to spew something back at the police officer when everybody in the car burst out laughing. Owen had befriended the cop at the show and had arranged the entire rib.

That was typical Owen Hart. He had a great sense of humor. He was constantly pulling practical jokes on people, whether they were wrestlers or not. One time Hacksaw Jim Duggan and his wife were in a hotel in another town that was also on the underside of the Mason-Dixon Line. They were looking for a place to work out, and Jim called down to the concierge to ask where the closest gym was located.

Well, the concierge had stepped away from his desk and it was Owen Hart who answered the phone—complete with a counterfeit English accent. He sounded like Arthur Treacher trying to hawk fish and chips,

When Hacksaw asked about the nearest gym, Owen asked Jim if he had a phone book in the room. Jim said he did, but since they did not know the town very well, they did not where the addresses were located.

That's when Owen asked Jim if he was one of the wrestlers who was staying in the hotel. When Jim said yes, Owen went on to talk about how stupid wrestlers were. I think he made a reference to our collective IQs—and the grand total was none too impressive.

Jim was incensed. While not all wrestlers are Mensa members, Duggan had in fact gotten his degree in applied plant biology at Southern Methodist University. He was definitely no dummy. He told Owen not to move, that he would be right down to the hotel lobby.

By the time Hacksaw got downstairs, the real concierge had returned to his desk. Suddenly, there was Hacksaw Jim Duggan screaming at him. The poor guy never had a clue.

This next rib might cause the Humane Society to press charges. It will definitely make both vegetarians and PETA members gag.

It was customary that when someone moved into your wrestling territory, you would help him out. There is a brotherhood that exists among wrestlers. Mr. Fuji was a great guy, but he went over the top with some of his practical jokes. One particular wrestler said that he had to live in Hawaii for a while. Mr. Fuji, who was from Hawaii, had put all of his furniture in storage there because he was on the road. He told the other wrestler that he was more than welcome to use it and how to get it out of storage.

When it was time for that wrestler to leave Hawaii, he stole all of Mr. Fuji's furniture as a rib. Mr. Fuji was furious. A couple of months later, he invited the wrestler over to his house for a barbecue. When the guy came over, Mr. Fuji explained that his family had already eaten, but that he'd be happy to fix the guy a plate. After the wrestler had eaten his fill and told Mr. Fuji how delicious everything was, Mr. Fuji brought out a dog's head, complete with its skin and fur. The wrestler who had temporarily swiped Mr. Fuji's furniture had just dined on Fido. Or was it a barbequed Benji? I assumed the meal was properly salted, since Mr. Fuji was famous for throwing salt into the faces of other wrestlers.

At least that wrestler did not have to pay for the meal. Belatedly, I knew the feeling. It was 1968, and it was my first year wrestling in the Northeast. Lou Albano and Tony Altimore were wrestling there too, and we all became good friends. They both were real characters.

Tony had been a dispatcher for a taxicab company and Lou had been one of his drivers. Tony wound up competing in the WWWF for nearly 16 years and was a solid mid-card wrestler in the 1960s and held the WWWF tag titles in the late 1960s. Lou had gone to the University of Tennessee and was a very good football player.

Tony and Lou achieved some success as a tag team called the Sicilians. They were the stereotypical Italian gangster duo, and were good enough to win the Midwest tag team championship in 1961 at Comiskey Park in Chicago.

Tony and Lou had a car and I did not, so I rode with them every day. They were my transportation, and I would pay for gas. Every time we stopped to eat, they told me that I was a guest and that they were buying my meal.

This went on all summer. I paid for gas and they paid for food. But when it was time for me to go back to Michigan to teach and coach, they handed me a bag with 40 to 50 restaurant tabs in it. It turns out they hadn't been paying for any of my meals. Instead, they let me walk out without paying all summer long. It turns out there were probably a whole lot of Howard Johnson restaurants with wanted posters of me taped next to the cash registers.

Restaurants were not the only entities being shortchanged in the Northeast. One ring announcer, who we called Koogie, was an Irish-Italian guy who all of us loved. He was a certifiable Boston character, a chubby old guy who walked with a cane. During shows, the midgets would sneak underneath the ring and cut about ¼ inch off Koogie's cane every night. By the time we left Boston, he would be walking on that cane like the Hunchback of Notre Dame.

Then again, a bent-over Koogie was definitely not the worst thing any of us had ever seen in or around a wrestling ring. It was in either 1986 or 1987 when Don Muraco and I wrestled in a charity event in a high school in Pennsylvania. The referee that night had the worst looking toupee I had ever seen in my life. I mean, it looked like somebody had shot a muskrat and plopped it on his head. Either that, or a coyote had come out on the wrong end of a match with a Peterbilt.

Don and I had a plan. We got locked up really tight and stayed that way until the ref had to come in and break us up. When he got close to us, I reached over and ripped the wig off his head. It was glued on really tight. I might have gotten some skin, too, but once it came off I put it on my head and did my crazy dance. The fans loved it.

The referee certainly did not share their enjoyment. He turned all kinds of colors. He was very angry and after the match he got right up in my face in the locker room. Finally, I figured out what was going on: he had a girl with him that night who he was trying to impress. I had to tell him that if she was with him because of his hair, he was really in trouble. Don and I were roaring with laughter, and the more we laughed the madder he got.

While the ref did not start crying that night, that was not the case during a rib by Crybaby George Cannon. George was a very big, very heavy guy who could produce tears on command. That was just one of his talents. George could go from laughter to Niagara Falls in about 3.5 seconds.

There were four of us in a car, and George was driving way too fast. We were coming home from a show in Grand Rapids, Michigan, and the next thing you know, the sirens were blaring and the lights were flashing and George was getting pulled over for speeding.

Even though the police officer told George to stay in the car, George got right out and told us he'd handle it.

As soon as the officer approached, George started crying. Even though we knew they were counterfeit tears, the cop did not have any idea what he was in for. A sniffling George started bawling and said this was a horrible way for a horrible night to end. George proceeded to tell the officer that we had been in Grand Rapids and had done a wrestling show to raise money for a police officer who had been killed in the line of duty. We were trying to raise money so the officer's family would have a nice Christmas, and now that he would have to pay for a speeding ticket, his own family would not have a nice Christmas because there would be no money. By the time his Academy Award–winning performance was over, the cop was patting George on the back and apologizing for even pulling him over. Needless to say, Crybaby did not get a ticket.

While I was never a crybaby, I very nearly felt like one when I became the object of a rib. There were four of us on the road in Texas. It was 1986 or 1987 and everybody was talking about snakes. I made the mistake of telling the other guys that I hated snakes. Somebody mentioned that either Kerry or Kevin Von Erich used to like to catch rattlesnakes, milk them so there was no venom, and then hide them in somebody's suitcase for a practical joke.

We stopped at a truck stop that resembled the Bates Motel. I had to go to the bathroom, and they told me the only one was in the back. I unzipped my pants just before I stepped into the outhouse, and when the door started to close I could hear the whirring of a rattlesnake. I was petrified. I stood there with a death grip on my manhood, much too frightened to move. While it seemed like an hour, I was probably frozen like that for 10 minutes or so until the guys came out of the truck stop and began shouting, "George, are you all right?" I told them to be quiet, that there was a rattlesnake inside with me. They told me to get ready, and that they would open the door, and I should run outside as fast as I could. There I went, with my manhood flopping like a smallmouth bass just yanked from the lake, hustling away from that outhouse. As it turned out, there was no snake at all. An old spring on the door started vibrating every time the door opened. It sure sounded just like a snake's rattle to me.

CHAPTER 10
The Savage Beast

Ever read the comic strip *The Lockhorns*? It is about the trials and tribulations of a married couple, Leroy and Loretta. Sure, there is a little bliss involved. But there are also a couple of cups of aggravation mixed with two tablespoons of irritation. Such was the story of my nearly two-year run with Randy "Macho Man" Savage.

We were, in essence, like a married couple. Not in a conjugal visit sort of way. Not in a wedding chapel in Las Vegas sort of way. Not like Ellen and Portia. Or Ozzie and Harriet. After all, we were both already married. Me, to my lovely wife, Pat. Randy, to the lovely Miss Elizabeth.

But Randy and I spent so much time together that it sometimes felt as if we were married. We were in the ring together almost non-stop for nearly two years. We wrestled and we bickered. We joked and we jostled. We punched and pulled. We poked and prodded. All in all, it was a very successful run.

There was also jealousy—often more real than imagined.

Randy was a tremendous athlete, a great wrestler, and an amazing heel. He was definitely one of the industry's greatest champions. During his career, he held 20 titles and six world championships.

For most of career, he was managed by Elizabeth Hulette, his wife in real life, who was known in wrestling circles as the lovely Miss Elizabeth. He always entered the ring with "Pomp and Circumstance" playing in the background. He broke into wrestling in 1973.

His ring personality was that of a crazed, ego-driven bully who treated Miss Elizabeth poorly but threatened anyone who even looked at her. Our feud began on the January 4, 1986, edition of *Saturday Night's Main Event.* That is when my well-known crush on Miss Elizabeth took hold. Then again, *everybody* loved Elizabeth. She was gorgeous, and wonderful at portraying the epitome of innocence. Her facial expressions were priceless. She felt sorry for me because of the way I was.

Vince did not know Randy and I had already faced one another in the ring some years earlier in Akron. I put a pretty good licking on Randy, and afterward I thanked him.

I had known Randy's dad, Angelo Poffo. We had wrestled at some shows together in Michigan and Ohio in the early days. I used to see Randy once in a while back then, when was just a young kid.

Angelo Poffo died in March 2010. He had a nice career in wrestling. He won a title and is a member of the WCW Hall of Fame. He was also an upstanding gentleman. He was very religious and rarely drank other than the occasional glass of red wine. Still, his sons would became his greatest legacy. Their ring names were Randy "Macho Man" Savage and "Leaping" Lanny Poffo.

"I have always been proud to call Angelo Poffo my father," Randy wrote in an e-mail to the *St. Petersburg Times* following his father's death. "He is a great example of a self-sacrificing, hardworking man who always put his family first. He has always been my hero and my mentor, and the priceless gifts he gave me I will have and cherish forever."

As a 20-year-old seaman, Angelo set a world record for consecutive sit-ups when he somehow managed to do 6,033. Breaking the record took more than four hours. A devout Catholic, he planned on doing just 6,000 situps but opted for 33 more, one for every year of Jesus' lifetime.

When Vince brought us together years later, Randy immediately started talking about that early match we'd had back in Akron. He said that he thought I was mad at him because I beat him up so badly and then said thanks. I just laughed and told him that was just the way I wrestled. A lot of guys did not want anything to do with me in the ring. I took things pretty seriously, especially when I was just starting out.

Before our first encounter in the WWF, I handed a bouquet of flowers to Elizabeth. While it was scripted, Randy did not like that part of the plan one bit. He was really upset. I did not know about his jealousy until then. During the match, Randy whipped me with the flowers. Let me tell you, those stems might as well have been leather bullwhips. I felt like one of the bad guys on the wrong end of Clint Eastwood's malice in *High Plains Drifter*. At one point in the match I got tied up in the ropes, and Randy kept on whipping me. This was no Valentine's Day bouquet, it was the St. Valentine's Day Massacre. I finally got free just as Randy got onto the top rope, waving the flower stems above his head in victory. I was mighty ticked off, and there was nothing counterfeit about that. I reached up, grabbed him by the pants, and yanked him down. He landed with a thud. Here it was, only our first match, and we'd already had our first spat. The Lockhorns in wrestling garb. I was really irritated. I was full of welts from getting whipped by the flower stems. So much for any endorsement deal with FTD.

Truth be told, Vince had no real long-term plans for Randy and me. None of us knew how our feud would go over. Randy was the heel and I had become a loveable cartoon character. It soon became apparent the possibilities were endless, and most of them revolved around Miss Elizabeth.

George "the Animal" Steele was smitten with her. Of course, my ring character could not express his emotions very well. Give me a crayon and some paper and, in character, I couldn't draw a heart. Give me the opportunity, and I couldn't say "I love you," even with the Rosetta Stone. Randy played the part of an enraged husband very well. Some might say he was typecast.

Typically, we would be in the middle of a heated match when, all of a sudden, I would stare, owl-eyed, at Elizabeth. I would go from hammering Randy to ham-handedly approaching Elizabeth. I might go over and stroke her hair the way a child might pet a Labrador retriever. That would incense Randy. He would jump off the top rope and clobber me. He would blast me with a chair. He would come from behind and hit me with a haymaker that could have taken a Clydesdale to its knees. Randy would then scoop Elizabeth up and hustle her out of harm's way. To Randy, my name was harm.

I remember prior to an event in Tampa, we spent a lot of time on outtakes that would be shown during the televised match. In one, we were at a water park, and Randy was teaching Elizabeth how to swim. They both were on a diving deck, and he pushed her into the pool. She was screaming mad, and I am not certain that part had been agreed upon. At the same time, I was in the kiddie pool surrounded by beautiful models. It was Beauties and the Beast, and the Beast was starting to sweat profusely. Nothing is more attractive than a bald head beaded by perspiration. So, I went down a slide that was all of about four feet long. Once I splashed into the pool, I grabbed a rubber duck and kept saying "Duckie." Johnny Depp, eat your heart out.

The match itself was held in an arena on the campus of the University of South Florida. Randy showed up in the locker room with a script that was probably four or five pages long. I felt like he wanted me to audition for something by Scorsese. What was this, pro wrestling or Broadway? Now, I was an old-school guy. I learned about the business in the backseats of cars going to and coming back from shows in places like Kalamazoo and Muskegon. I learned from the likes of Crusher Cortez and Leaping Larry Chene. I went to school between bites of bologna sandwiches and swigs of beer. The class was called Wrestling 101, and everything was impromptu. There were no scripted scenarios, there were only instincts. Everything we did was to get heat on our opponent. You'd back off just before a riot broke out, and then turn the knob on the stove again to get it reheated. You played the crowd like Pee Wee Herman played a Stradivarius (or was that a bicycle horn?). I'd been wrestling since the 1960s, and this was 1986. To be honest, I took offense to what Randy was proposing. So I pretended to read the first page, slowly crumpled the paper, and tossed it into the trash can. I did the same thing with the rest of the pages, very slowly and very deliberately. All the while, Randy was going ballistic. I just told him to calm down, listen to me in the ring, and we'd have a great match. What's that old saying—what goes over in L.A. might not work in Peoria? That was exactly how I felt.

You can't teach an old Animal new tricks. I was nearly 50 years old. I was on another sort of slide, and this one was not into a kiddie pool. It was my career as a wrestler. I was two decades older than a lot of the other guys in the locker room, including Randy. In a ring full of chiseled bodies, I was not all sharp angles. I looked like I'd come out of a Jell-O mold. Any reference to six packs had more to do with Stroh's or Pabst's than abs. I looked a lot more like the guy sitting in the 21st row than I did somebody that Michelangelo sculpted.

There was nothing wrong with Randy's approach; he was just being a professional. Me, I was being a hardhead and I took it the wrong way. He was part of wrestling's future and he was getting a big push. There were big plans for him. Meanwhile, I was becoming part of wrestling's past. George "the Animal" Steele was in wrestling's rearview mirror. My ways were becoming past tense. Eventually, Randy and I compromised. While we never choreographed a single one of our many matches, we repeated a lot of things that had worked well in the past.

While Randy was always very professional, having Elizabeth there made things tough for him. I think it would have been tough for anyone. She was a beautiful young lady. They were married, and it was never easy having your wife with you on the road. Most of the guys I knew who tried it wound up divorced, and they were no exception. Professional wrestling was not exactly the set of *The Waltons*. Sometimes, the only thing warm and fuzzy about it was the hair on my chest and back. There was always something going on that would raise his hackles. When Randy and Miss Elizabeth would walk to the ring, people would reach out to touch her. Randy was constantly yelling at the security guards to keep the fans bank.

Once we were wrestling at Joe Louis Arena in Detroit. Randy beat me via a count-out when he hit me with a lifeguard chair. That's where Elizabeth had been sitting. The pre-match stipulation was that the winner would walk away with Elizabeth as his manager. After I'd lost the match, I hugged a poster of Elizabeth in the middle of the ring.

Prior to the match, the Junkyard Dog had been ribbing Randy. He said that when Elizabeth was sitting on the lifeguard chair, I would be looking right up Elizabeth's dress whenever I was on my back. Everybody had a good laugh—everybody but Randy, that is.

Honestly, Randy was the most jealous man I had ever met, and it created a real problem. Was his love for Elizabeth as strong as his love for money? Our whole schtick was built around me being smitten over Miss Elizabeth and Randy being jealous. I had to keep reminding Randy that not only was I married, but I had a daughter who was older than Miss Elizabeth.

One night I put her over my shoulder and ran out of the arena with her. When we were all back in the locker room, Randy started shouting, "What are they going to think that George is doing to my wife?"

Another night in Detroit, Vince McMahon asked me to grab Miss Elizabeth by the ankle. You guessed it, Randy went R.P. McMurphy crazy. We were not flying over the cuckoo's nest; we were living in it. Every night it was something different. Randy's jealousy was driving him crazy. There were times when he would lock her in the dressing room. Randy was always screaming at somebody.

Believe me, Randy was not the only wrestler out there with an ego as fragile as porcelain. Wrestling is a make believe business, and the stars are never truly in control of their own success. Plenty of superstars had a hard time reconciling reality with what they portrayed in the ring. Beneath the loud and brash exterior of most professional wrestlers resides an unbelievably insecure person, and that is the way the bosses want it.

The wrestling business is constructed on total subjectivity. How tough a person happens to be, or how legitimate his wrestling skills are, often have absolutely nothing to do with his or her success. Sure, certain physical characteristics help. While Hulk Hogan took complete advantage of his looks and charisma, Sid Vicious did not. But the bottom line is that success is not up to the individual wrestler.

It was the McMahons who determined success or failure. First, it was Mr. McMahon; now it is Vince McMahon. This not unique to the WWWF, the WWF, or the WWE. It is just how the business works.

There is no other business that I know of in which success has more to do with what I call "office politics." The office decides, based on different factors, who will get the push and who will not. So what are those factors? Unfortunately, they are pretty much like a cell phone plan—family and friends.

If you're the boss, your position is there for eternity. Marry the boss' daughter and your position will solidify. Be the boss' kid and your job security is ironclad. Be the boss' buddy and you will find steady work. That is the way it works in a lot of businesses. Just ask the Fords, the Vanderbilts, or the Kennedys.

Professional wrestling has always been a business of independent contractors. There is no security, no union, no insurance, and no pension. There is nothing except your position in the organization.

I occupied a unique place in the business. I was a part-time employee with a full-time reputation. I was a teacher and a coach, but I was also a professional wrestler. I understood early on how to give George "the Animal" Steele a good position. I understood how George fit into a promotion, and because of that I was a solid draw and a performer for many years. I also always understood the importance of keeping Jim and George separate. That was done both for family reasons and sanity reasons. I wanted the couch that I reclined on to be my own, not owned by some therapist charging $150 per hour.

Randy and I went at it for nearly two years. All of the matches were memorable in their own way. At my age, I was fortunate to be part of such a great run.

On February 17, 1986, at Madison Square Garden, WWF world champion Hulk Hogan pinned Randy after Hogan hit a legdrop for the win.

At WrestleMania, Randy pinned me at 7:08 using both feet on the ropes for leverage. Late in the contest, I kicked out of his flying elbow smash. After the bout, I chased the referee backstage.

On July 26, 1986, in the Spectrum in Philadelphia, Randy defeated me via disqualification at 5:29 after I refused to stop choking him with the champion's own weapon.

In August 1986 at the Boston Garden, Hulk Hogan and I defeated Randy and Adrian Adonis at 10:28 when Hogan pinned Adonis with the legdrop after Savage accidentally backdropped his partner and was knocked to the floor.

Back at the Boston Garden a month later, Randy beat me via disqualification when I threw a number of chairs into the ring, one of which hit the champion. After the match, he returned to the ring twice and I attacked him on both occasions. Police officers and officials finally had to break us up.

In Toronto, Randy beat me again when I was disqualified at 3:48 after taking his foreign object and using it on him. After the bout, I chased him backstage before returning to the ramp and slamming the champion. After hearing the official decision from the ring announcer, I chased Randy backstage once more.

In Hartford in December 1986, I got pinned after Randy hit me with the timekeeper's bell. During the bout, Ricky Steamboat came to ringside. Moments later, I carried Elizabeth backstage. Ricky was then escorted from ringside by referees and security, and I returned to the ring. After the bout, Ricky returned to the ring to save me just as Randy prepared to smash the ring bell into my throat.

WrestleMania III, at the Silverdome in Pontiac, Michigan, marked the end of my run with Randy. Randy and Ricky had been feuding for six months—since Randy attacked Ricky by leaping off the top rope and battering his throat with the ring bell. Their WrestleMania III match lasted about 15 minutes, but many of the 93,000-plus in the Silverdome that night swore it was longer. Both Randy and Ricky were outstanding athletes. I was in Steamboat's corner and Miss Elizabeth was in Randy's corner. Ricky won the Intercontinental title with a little assistance on my part—I pushed Randy off the top rope as he was about to jump off and hit Steamboat with the timekeeper's bell.

That battle was voted Match of the Year by the *Wrestling Observer Newsletter* and *Pro Wrestling Illustrated*. It remains one of the best matches in the history in pro wrestling. The main event that night was Hulk Hogan against Andre the Giant. Their characters had been good friends—at least on the surface. But the story line was that Andre did not like being overshadowed by Hulk, and those feelings bubbled over on an episode of Piper's Pit. Andre was given a trophy for his 15-year undefeated streak and Hogan received a larger trophy for his three-year tenure as champ. Andre listened to Hulk drone on during his acceptance speech and then he finally walked out. When Andre next appeared on Piper's Pit, he was with his new manager, Bobby "the Brain" Heenan. The beloved Andre the Giant had become a giant heel. In reality, Andre was nearing the end of his career and had been convinced by Vince McMahon to play the bad guy.

WrestleMania III set an indoor attendance record of 93,173, only recently broken by the 2010 NBA All-Star Game at Cowboys Stadium. More than $1.5 million was generated in ticket sales alone. Another million viewers watched at 160 closed-circuit locations in North America, and several million more were watching via pay-per-view. That totaled an estimated $10 million in revenue. Those numbers were hard to grasp for everyone, let alone a guy who got into the business originally because he was making $4,300 as a teacher and a coach.

That two-year run with Randy was a phenomenal time and I was fortunate to be a part of it. Randy went on to become WWF world champion, replacing Hulk Hogan for a time.

Sadly, Randy died on May 20, 2011, after suffering a heart attack while driving with his second wife, Lynn Payne, in Seminole, Florida. He lost control of his Jeep Wrangler and crashed into a tree. An autopsy found he had an enlarged heart and advanced coronary artery disease. Lynn suffered minor injuries.

"He had so much life in his eyes and in his spirit, I just pray that he's happy and in a better place and we miss him," fellow wrestler Hulk Hogan wrote on Twitter. "We miss him a lot. I feel horrible about the 10 years of having no communication. This was a tough one."

Looking back, Randy "Macho Man" Savage was the ultimate perfectionist. His career was really taking off at the time, while mine was winding down. I truly believe there was not a better wrestler for me to close out my career with. My heart was heavy the day that Randy had his fatal accident.

Randy's first wife, Elizabeth Hulette and pro wrestling's Miss Elizabeth, died of an overdose in 2003. (She and Randy had divorced back in 1992.) Elizabeth's death shocked me. She was living with Lex Luger at the time. When Lex Luger came to the WWF, I was an agent. He had a tremendous body, a great look, and he got a big push. We called him "the Narcissist." He had little or no respect for me or anyone else in authority, so I had a very hard time liking Lex Luger.

They tried to make a big star out of him. We put him in a blimp that traveled across the country. His potential was better than his performance. He made millions on potential alone, in my opinion.

On April 19, 2003, Lex Luger was involved in a domestic dispute with Elizabeth in the garage of their townhouse in Marietta, Georgia. Luger allegedly struck her, and Cobb County police found Elizabeth with two bruised eyes, a bump on her head, and a cut lip. He was charged with battery and released on $2,500 bond.

Two days later, he was arrested for DUI after he rear-ended another car. According to the police report, Luger had slurred speech, bloodshot eyes, and could not locate a driver's license. He also had a handgun in the car, which was illegal in Georgia. Elizabeth, a passenger in the vehicle, was sent home in a taxi. Luger had been driving with a suspended license.

On May 1, 2003, Elizabeth died in that same townhouse after mixing pills of hydrocodone, Xanax, and anabolic steroids with vodka. Luger was arrested later that day after the police found anabolic steroids, OxyContin, synthetic growth hormone, testosterone, and alprazolam in the townhouse. He was charged with 14 drug possession counts, 13 of them felonies. He received a $1,000 fine and five years' probation and would not have gone to jail had he not violated the terms of his probation. But in 2005, he was picked up on a flight from Minneapolis to Canada. Under the terms of his probation, he was not allowed to leave the country. He was sentenced to nine weeks in prison.

While incarcerated, Luger met a chaplain who would bring him chunky peanut butter for some extra protein. That small favor from Steve Baskin, the pastor of Western Hills Baptist Church in Kennesaw, Georgia, led to discussions about the Lord. Lex acknowledged he had been a narcissistic jerk. When I was an agent, he would either downright reject anything I asked him to do, or do it in his own sweet time.

In 2008, Lex Luger accepted the Lord Jesus Christ as his personal savior. He was slated to attend an Athletes in Action gathering in Phoenix. I was still so upset about the death of Miss Elizabeth and his narcissistic attitude that I did not want to be around him. I told my wife, Pat, that we could not go to Phoenix as planned, but she reminded me not to let anyone stand between me and the Lord.

When we got to Arizona, Pat and I signed in at the main desk in the hotel. While we were walking down the hall, Lex turned and we ran smack-dab into each other. We literally made physical contact. I put my arms around him and he patted me on my back. He had tears in his eyes. I told him I would see him later.

Two days later, at a church in Phoenix, Lex and I stood at the pulpit in front of thousands of people as Lex gave his testimony. All the while, he was sobbing.

In fact, we both had tears in our eyes. I was crying for Miss Elizabeth. But I was also crying for Lex Luger's salvation. While Lex certainly was not the thief on the cross, he was definitely the narcissist on the wrestling mat.

I had been no angel myself for a long time. Whenever you're in the spotlight, the tendency is to believe that the light emanates from within yourself. That's self-absorption, and if it is not a sin, it certainly can lead to many of them. While I did not break every one of the commandments during my time in wrestling, I certainly put hairline fissures in a few of them. It took me quite some time to find the Lord. It wasn't as if He was hiding; I just hadn't bothered to look.

CHAPTER 11

A Potpourri of Perspiration

This chapter is going to contain a little bit of this and some of that. These stories compose something of a patchwork quilt of my many years inside and outside of professional wrestling. It will offer some behind-the-scenes stuff, as well as some in-front-of-the-camera perspective.

Einhorn's Incursion

In the summer of 1975, Eddie Einhorn's International Wrestling Association (IWA) started to throw some elbows and thump its chest in the New York City area. Einhorn, who is now a minority owner of the Chicago White Sox, is no lightweight, so Mr. McMahon had to pay attention.

Einhorn has been involved with Major League Baseball for more than three decades, most of that time with the White Sox. He is in his sixth decade in the sports and broadcasting industry. He is also on the board of directors for the Chicago Bulls. He is recognized as the architect of baseball's first billion-dollar television contract.

While wrestling didn't promise anything close to a billion dollars in the mid-1970s, there was still the potential for a lot of money to be made. Einhorn made a deal with WOR (Channel 9) while Mr. McMahon and the WWWF were stuck on the Spanish-language WNJU (Channel 47) at midnight. Not exactly a prime spot for programming or advertisers.

I had never seen Mr. McMahon so upset. Einhorn scheduled a show at Roosevelt Stadium featuring IWA champion Mil Mascaras against former WWWF champion Ivan Koloff. That show was on Friday night, and Mr. McMahon's WWWF show was set for Saturday night across the river at Madison Square Garden. I was scheduled to wrestle champion Bruno Sammartino at the WWWF show.

The star-studded IWA show killed our advance sales. Frankly, they had a better card than we did. But Mario Savoldi and some others from the WWWF bought cheap tickets and raided the ringside seats at the IWA show. Mario's father had been an agent for Mr. McMahon. They caused a lot of chaos and it turned into a very scary situation. The fans at the IWA show were not happy. The New Jersey State Athletic Association did not make things any easier for Einhorn's group, either. All of this, plus some lousy weather, killed Einhorn's IWA show.

Something else helped kill the IWA show, and this is something that I never told Mr. McMahon when he was alive or Vince, for that matter. Crybaby George Cannon, who was a friend of mine at the time, had called and asked to show up at Roosevelt Stadium and be introduced as a new member of the IWA. The IWA was really going for the jugular, and Crybaby Cannon said they did not want me to show up the following night at Madison Square Garden for my match with Bruno.

I told him that I would not do that. The McMahons had been good to me and my family and I owed them my loyalty. I knew Mr. McMahon had been under a lot of stress. The IWA had been putting on shows in different areas of the country, and if it managed to capture the New York market, that could have been it for the WWWF.

While we had a very poor advance for the WWWF show at MSG the next night, we still sold out. The IWA actually had a much stronger card for their Friday night show, but things did not work out the way they thought. I think they only drew about 14,000.

Bruno Sammartino was the heart of the WWWF. I was just a summer commodity, because in the fall I went back to school to teach and coach. But I was still a stronger draw than most; Mr. McMahon could bring me in for a few visits, but I could shoot 12 television shows during that time. We'd do some sold-out shows, and then they would not have to pay me again until the following summer.

The IWA was brand new, but Einhorn was a powerful guy because of his television contacts. He was using wrestling like a toy. I think he saw the potential, just like Vince did. Einhorn was offering guys more money, free transportation in and out of shows, and free hotel rooms. But after the IWA's New York City debacle, Einhorn's organization began to die a slow death. If they had gotten a foothold in New York, who knows what would have happened?

Independent Thinking

As my days as an agent with the WWF were coming to an end, the Honky Tonk Man started to fill me in on the independent wrestling business. I did not have a clue about it at that time. He told me to put my name out there and see what happened. I mean, I was 61 years old by then. I wasn't with the WWF, I was with AARP. But people still felt a lot of nostalgia for George "the Animal" Steele. So, I would get into the ring and do a few spots, eat a turnbuckle pad or two, and the fans would go nuts. That says a lot about the loyalty of our great fans. They were still cheering a guy munching turnbuckles when he should have been munching prunes and Fiber One.

We had a couple of sellouts in Sacramento and the word began to travel fast. All of a sudden, I was in great demand in independent wrestling circles. It was a blast from the past. This was golf's senior tour, as far as I was concerned, only this particular Tom Watson was wearing wrestling boots and not FootJoys.

When I broke into the wrestling business back in Michigan in 1962, the landscape was much different. The country was divided into territories, and they each had their own promotions and shows. Bert Ruby was my mentor. He was also a sensational Jewish light heavyweight wrestler, legendary promoter, and host of TV's *Motor City Wrestling*.

Independent wrestling has replaced those territories. There is a wide gap among all the different independent promotions in terms of how they conduct their business. There are some outstanding independent promotions, and others that I don't approve of, like the ones depicted in the movie *The Wrestler*, starring Mickey Rourke. When I am invited to an independent wrestling promotion, the very first question I ask is if their promotion is family friendly. If it isn't, I do not want anything to do with it. I love meeting the young folks who dream about a career in professional wrestling.

Most independent wrestling promotions treat the established guys, aka old wrestlers, with great respect. Most young wrestlers will come up and introduce themselves with a firm handshake. The young guys have a ton of questions and love it when I watch their matches and give them my opinion. I believe most of today's superstars got their start in the independent promotions.

Here is how it works for us so-called legends: everything is agreed upon long before the actual wrestling event takes place. The legend is picked up at the airport and taken to a hotel. Later, he's picked up at the hotel and taken to the event. Most promotions pay the legend upon his arrival. The legend then does everything in his power to have a positive impact for the promoters. After the show, the promoters either take the legend out on the town, or maybe just treat him to a meal and then take him back to the hotel. At my age, it has been further reduced to warm milk and cookies, and that is fine with me. It is a good night for both parties; there is certainly not a lot of stress for me.

I have had so many great experiences at independent wrestling shows, but there is one in particular that stands out. Cindie Hall was promoting a show near Lansing, Michigan, that I had agreed to be part of, and her booker sent me a plane ticket that had me flying out of Tampa. For those of you who excel at geography like I did back at Madison High School, Tampa and Cocoa Beach do not exactly occupy the same block in Florida. One is on the Atlantic side—that is where I live; Tampa is on the Gulf Coast side. I was not about to drive across the state to catch a flight, so I planned to cancel out of the show. But then I got a call from Cindie and she proceeded to tell me how important it was to her that I make an appearance. Cindie told me that the only reason she promoted wrestling shows was for her son, Josh. She told me that Josh loved watching wrestling on television, and that he loved to ring the bell to start the matches for his favorite wrestlers. Josh had been born with spina bifida and was paralyzed from the waist. He wanted to ring the bell to start my match. When I heard that, I immediately said I'd be at the show. I was amazed when I met Josh and Cindie. Josh had taken his George "the Animal" Steele action figure to the hospital for comfort when he was about to go in for one of his many surgeries. Josh and Cindie have touched me in so many positive ways over the years. Pat and I love them both and feel like they are part of our extended family.

Eventually, mostly because of my battle with Crohn's disease, getting into the ring is no longer a possibility. I now do a lot of personal appearances that include question-and-answer sessions, autograph signings, and occasionally standing in someone's corner.

Fans still have an opportunity to spend time and talk with many different legends at these kinds of events. There is also an opportunity for fans to get autographed pictures of their favorite wrestlers. The point is for everyone to have fun and enjoy themselves.

Personal appearances are pretty much like wrestling on the independent scene—minus the wrestling. It's a great way for me to get to know more about the fans who have been so loyal all of these years. While every personal appearance is special, some are more memorable than others. In August 2012, I threw out the first pitch at Fenway Park in Boston. It was part of the 100th anniversary of the venerable stadium, and I had wrestled there in the past.

Of course, I did not just simply throw out a pitch. I had to do it up in George "the Animal" Steele style. I doctored the ball, bit it in front of the sold-out crowd, and grabbed some stuffing between my teeth. The people in Boston went wild.

I also love working minor league baseball games. First, I have a great respect for and enjoy the game of baseball. Remember, I played in high school. My style probably would not have been wholeheartedly endorsed by Abner Doubleday. When I played first base, the percentage of guys who rounded the bag without at least stumbling was on the low side. Minor league baseball is very fun and family friendly. The prices for tickets and concessions are low enough for a family to enjoy itself without having to take a second mortgage on the house. I even made the ESPN Top 10 highlights one day after throwing out the first pitch for the Rochester (NY) Red Wings. Of course, it was a George "the Animal" Steele flutter ball, complete with flapping leather and billowing stuffing.

George "the Animal" Steele Jr.

Pat and I have three great kids of our own and more than a handful of grandchildren whom we love dearly. But I am Jim Myers. George "the Animal" Steele did not have a family. He was born in the wild and raised by a pack of wolves—or was it yeti? He did not have a herd, a litter, or a pack to call his own.

I was chatting with Matt Bloom at an independent show just outside of Boston one night. Matt was 6'5", 300 pounds, and a high school football coach. We seemed to have a lot in common.

Matt claimed he had more body hair than I did. I laughed, and asked him if he was a yak. We both laughed.

That night, I was sound asleep in my hotel room when I awoke with a start. The alarm clock said 4:00 AM and yet I was wide awake. A great story line had hit me like a Randy Savage haymaker. What if George "the Animal" Steele had a bastard son from one bad night gone definitely wrong in Brooklyn? That bastard son was Matt Bloom, who would be known as George "the Animal" Steele Jr. He hated his father because he had been abandoned. At the same time, a part of Junior loved his father and wanted to follow in his footsteps and become a professional wrestler. He carried two George "the Animal" Steele action figures; one that he kept spit-shined and wrapped in silk, and one that was full of bite marks and almost completely torn apart. The action figures represented love and hate. George Jr. would be more messed up than his father. Just lay down on the couches, George and George Jr. The psychiatrist will be with you in just a minute.

The next night I was still in the Boston area, for another show. I was excited when I found out that Matt Bloom was also booked on the show. When he showed up, I asked Matt if he would like to become my "son" and work for the WWE. Matt got excited and really liked the idea. I told him we had a lot to work to do, because he wasn't exactly ready for the WWE yet. I called Vince McMahon at his home and ran the story line by him. He loved it. A few days later, Jim Ross called and we talked about my bastard son idea becoming reality. Jim Ross asked me how much money it would take to get the idea off and running. We kicked it around, J.R. would not make an offer, and I finally pitched $200,000 each for both Matt and myself.

A couple of weeks later, I got a call from Jim Ross inviting Matt and me to Stamford to meet with Vince. Before we went, I told Matt about

Vince's office and what to expect. Behind the desk was a picture frame which contained only a bright red cloth. When Vince McMahon sits at his desk, his head is backdropped by the picture frame. Red is a power color, and I told Matt I always believed it was there because Vince thought it gave him an edge during meetings.

The day of the meeting finally arrived and I fully expected to be put on hold for a couple of hours. Making people wait is just another mind game that Vince often plays. Much to my surprise, we were immediately given a tour of the office and hustled right into the meeting with Vince, the world's most successful promoter. Also in the office were Jim Ross and Bruce Prichard.

I thought Matt was going to lose it when he saw the framed red cloth behind Vince's head. After the friendly handshakes it was time to get down to business. The first thing Vince said was that he heard I had fallen out of the ring at an independent show and really hit my head hard. I laughed and said no, that did not happen. He then asked, if I hadn't landed on my head, how did I come up with the outrageous $200,000 figure? I looked Vince directly in the eyes and asked if he expected me to start negotiating at a low figure. After a lot of talk, it was decided that we would each be paid $1,000 a week, and Matt would be sent to Memphis to learn to work. It was honestly a sweet deal for all concerned.

Matt spent over a year training in Memphis, and I received my weekly check, waiting for big things to get started. In the process, Matt was searching for his personal identity. That does not mean he went looking for his fictional mama who resided in Brooklyn. The bastard son story line was obviously pure bunk. Matt had started piercing his face and body. When I first saw all of them, I laughingly asked Matt how would he ever get through security at airports. Still, I thought the piercings would fit into the generation-gap angle of the story. I thought the father-son story was really coming together and I was getting excited.

A little later, I got a phone call from Jim Ross. J.R. told me that Vince had made a creative change in his plans for Matt. Immediately, I knew the Junior story line had been put out to pasture. The phone sounded funny and I suspected I was on speaker. Ross asked me if I knew what a Prince Albert was. I said it was a can of tobacco. He said on the street, a Prince Albert was a penis piercing. I decided that I was not going to give them the pleasure of expressing my displeasure. I laughed and asked if they were telling George "the Animal" Steele that his form of family entertainment was being replaced by a pierced penis. I could tell they did not know how to respond. J.R. quickly told me that my next check at the end of the month would be my last and that Vince would be calling me soon. I knew that phone call would never come. But I found my own way to get closure on the night George "the Animal" Steele showed up at the WCW show in Buffalo, New York. That was my closure with Vince and the WWE. Believe me, it was a calculated decision. Free at last.

Who knows why they opted not to go with the George "the Animal" Steele Jr. story line? It might have been because Matt was still trying to find himself. I know he wrestled in Japan for about eight years, and is now with the WWE, wrestling as Tensai. Previously, between 1997 and 2004, he wrestled for the WWF/WWE as Prince Albert, Albert, and A-Train.

The Real Vince

Vince McMahon is a businessman. As his wealth grew, so did his notoriety. That is just the nature of the beast. The higher up you go, the more people grab a baseball and try to knock you into the dunk tank. Former wrestlers have knocked Vince for many different reasons. Fans have knocked Vince because they do not agree with the direction in which he has taken his business. He also gets knocked in the media.

Vince has gone out of his way to portray himself as a bad person, to make his family look dysfunctional. This has all been for business reasons. It is just another story line.

I believe you really find out what a person is like when you see him sweat, when his rear end is really on the line. I watched Vince react when he was accused of providing illegal steroids to wrestlers and put on trial in federal court. People were talking about him possibly serving time in jail. Former wrestlers took shots at Vince on talk shows. They were even talking about his personal life. The sharks were circling, and their teeth were sharp. He was a hunk of beef tenderloin treading water and you could see the fear in Vince's eyes and hear it in his voice. He was scared and very nervous.

That is when the true measure of Vince McMahon was exposed. That is when his father, Mr. McMahon, would have been the proudest.

I was at a meeting in which a high-profile lawyer tried to persuade WWF and Titan Sports to do a "We Are Righteous" campaign. The lawyer suggested very strongly that we publicize all of the positive things that we did as a company. He wanted to tell the story of the close contact the WWF and Titan Sports had with the Make-A-Wish foundation. He wanted to release all of the names of the children who had been in accidents or were suffering from some life-threatening illness whom we had helped.

Vince and his wife, Linda, replied that the WWF and Titan Sports did not support those charities for public relations. They refused to exploit those children to make the WWF and Titan Sports look good for some court case. Vince's father must have been smiling down at his son on that day.

The Halloran House

I was filming my first commercial for Minolta in New York City. If I recall correctly, the advertisement's theme was basically "So Simple Even The Animal Can Do It." Between growls and grunts and extremely quizzical looks at the camera, perhaps even I could push a button and come up with beautiful pictures.

There was a room reserved for me at the Halloran House on Lexington Avenue. It was kitty-corner from the famous Waldorf Astoria, a fancy place where they serve peanut butter sandwiches on silver platters and Nestlé's Quik in fine china.

The Halloran House was a mighty nice place, too. Even though George "the Animal" Steele was used to sleeping in caves surrounded by other wild animals, I could get used to the satin sheets and the suite that they put me in because of my late arrival. However, when I checked in that night, a very nice young lady at the front desk told me that I would need to move to a different room the very next day because the suite had been reserved. I told her no problem, and I meant it.

The next morning, Peter Demetrious, the hotel manager, called and was very apologetic when he repeated what I had been told about moving to another room. Peter said he'd be up with a bellhop to help me move. What I did not realize at the time was that he was a huge wrestling fan and had seen George "the Animal" Steele numerous times. Peter was frightened because he assumed my suite was probably already in shambles, with the stuffing ripped out of the mattress and the television tossed out the window and who knows what sort of other Animal-related mayhem.

When I opened the door, there were four bellhops and a man dressed in a suit. They were pressed against the wall across the hall. I think they were expecting the worst. If only I had known that Peter was expecting George "the Animal" Steele, I would have been in character. I would have chased the bellhops up and down the hallway. I would have lifted Peter over my head and slammed him on the bed. I would have ripped off my shirt and chewed off the buttons and slobbered and spit and done my routine the way I had done it so many times before, in front of packed arenas.

Instead, I opened the door and asked if I could help them. You would've thought I had just graduated from finishing school. I could not have been more polite, and Peter could not have been more relieved. Then and there we became fast friends.

George "the Animal" Steele immediately became a favored guest of the Halloran House, and I stayed there whenever I wrestled in the Big Apple. Normally the going rate was $300 and up per night. For years, wrestlers would have to move from one hotel to the other because something would happen. Someone would do something stupid, like break a couch or ruin a table or engage in a food fight, and pretty soon, wrestlers were not welcome anymore. They'd be told that no rooms were available, or the rates would suddenly rise so high that a Hubble telescope would be needed to see the rack card.

I told Peter about the problem and he agreed to give only the wrestlers that I recommended the great rate of $49 per night. I gave Peter a very short list of wrestlers because I did not want to lose the prestigious Halloran House as my hotel of choice. The list included guys like Bobby Heenan, Hillbilly Jim, and Greg Valentine—just a few guys with some class.

I had worked a show in Honolulu and came across a wrestler by the name of King Curtis. I gave him Vince McMahon's phone number. King Curtis was so beaten up that he could barely walk, but he could still talk on that microphone. King Curtis became "the Wizard," and Vince paired him with Kim Chee and Kimala the Ugandan Giant. I gave Peter the okay to add the Wizard to the preferred customer list at the Halloran House.

A couple of months later, in 1986, I had a sold-out match at Madison Square Garden. Peter was among the 19,000-plus fans in attendance and was sitting in the front row. I did a little cartoon stuff with Kamala and the fans were loving it, but the smiles turned to outrage when the Wizard caught me on the floor, with Kim Chee's help. They started doing a number on me. Eventually, the Ugandan Giant gave George Steele the big splash from the top rope to get the pin. He then added another splash, once again from the top rope, to add a little garnish to the conclusion of the match. Is there a doctor in the house? How about a chiropractor? I was hauled from the ring on a stretcher for the first time in my career. The entire arena got quiet and then it exploded in anger.

When the Wizard returned to the Halloran House, he found his room had been cleaned out. A bellhop had placed his luggage in the lobby. Thanks to his part in the performance at MSG, he had incited the rage of my good friend Peter Demetrious. The Wizard was no longer welcome at the Halloran House.

Annoucing a Change in Plans

Chasing ring announcer Gary Cappetta was not originally part of the act, but he got on the wrong side of the Animal in 1975 when he asked, "Where should I say you are from and how much should I say you weigh?" I did not like Gary's attitude and I chased him out of the locker room. That had happened a few times already, and Mr. McMahon was really starting to enjoy the scene.

One evening, as Gary began announcing my imminent arrival, I took off in a dead sprint toward the ring. As I got closer, I could see the fear in Cappetta's eyes, and it just spurred me on. As I went sliding into the ring in a move that would have made Lou Brock proud, Gary ran away from the microphone that dangled from the ceiling. As I raced after him, the microphone swung back and hit me in the head. The crowd went wild. As I grabbed him, he slid out of his tuxedo jacket and the straight pin that held the flower onto his lapel jammed deep into my hand. That only made me angrier. I can tell you, the crowd was going nuts.

From then on, I never talked to Gary Cappetta. We repeated that performance every time we crossed paths in an arena. He was very wary of me, and honestly, George "the Animal" Steele made a lot of ring announcers nervous. It was illegal for any of them to have a tranquilizer gun and that was about the only thing that would've kept me at bay. Years later, I met Gary in an airport and we had a good laugh about it.

Blade Runner

When I first got into the wrestling business, we were taught to protect every phase of it; it was called *kayfabe*. I never thought I'd be talking about blood, but times change and vampires have become extremely popular.

While the Cullens and Robert Pattinson have probably never climbed into a wrestling ring, they certainly know about blood. Blood did have a place in wrestling when used correctly, but I believe there were too many workers in the old days who depended on blood, also known as juice.

In the old days, the wrestlers got blood the hard way. If you hit the bone around the eye and twisted your fist on contact, chances were pretty good you would open up your opponent on the first punch and make him bleed. If you did not get him the first time, you continued to punch until you got the desired result. When you see blood in boxing or wrestling, it is usually coming from the eyes or the nose.

Later on, most everyone used blades.

The story goes that Wild Red Berry and Danny McShain were working with each other almost every night and selling out wherever they went. Their matches were wild and were often stopped because of the amount of blood being spilled. Some nights, it looked like an entire jug of strawberry Kool-Aid had been dumped over their heads. But Wild Red Berry and Danny McShain were not the only ones getting juice the hard way.

One summer, when my brother, Jack, wrestled with me in Pittsburgh, he could not believe that some guys would stand in front of mirrors to see how much blood they had flowing that night. It was a badge of honor for them, but it made Jack sick.

I remember the first time I used juice. I was just starting out and it was at a local match in Michigan. I'd been thrown out of the ring and it was time for me to bleed. Unfortunately, I had lost my blade, so the only option that occurred to me was to start beating my head against one of the metal posts holding up the ring. I looked like one of those crazies on the television show *Cops* who goes nuts and starts banging his head against the Plexiglas that separates the prisoner from the police officer in the police car. The blood eventually came and I was viewed as "one of the guys" from then on.

Another Sort of Punch

There are a few special moments that really stand out in my ever-weakening mind, and one is when Joe Louis, the former world heavyweight boxing champion from Detroit, refereed a match I had with Pedro Morales at Madison Square Garden. I remember sitting by the radio as a youngster and listening to his championship fights.

Joe Louis bolted onto the pro boxing scene in 1934 with a style and skill few had ever seen. Known as the "Brown Bomber," he emerged victorious from his first 27 fights, all but four of which he won via knockout.

While he was born in Alabama in 1914, his family moved to Detroit when he was 10, and that is when Joe became involved in boxing. Ten years after his arrival in the Motor City, he won the Golden Gloves as a light heavyweight. After that, he turned professional and began his rapid ascent in the heavyweight ranks.

He beat former champion Primo Carnera before a crowd of 62,000 at Yankee Stadium. He followed that with a fourth-round knockout of Max Baer. Seemingly invincible, he lost to Max Schmeling of Germany on June 19, 1936—a loss that stung for years to come. In 1937, Louis faced world heavyweight champion James J. Braddock in Chicago. Louis captured the heavyweight title of the world by knocking Braddock out in the eighth round. After this victory, Louis stated, "I don't want nobody to call me champ until I beat Schmeling." Louis had ascended to the top of the boxing world, but in his mind his journey was far from complete. His embarrassing loss to Max Schmeling was the only blemish on his career.

On June 22, 1938, Louis once again took on Schmeling, the only opponent who had ever beaten him. This time around, Louis knocked Schmeling out and captured the admiration of countless Americans. Louis gained a moral victory for himself and his country, and simultaneously struck a damaging symbolic blow to Hitler. Louis' first punches, a pair of powerful left hooks, belied his opponent's eventual demise. Schmeling complained bitterly about being hit with foul kidney punches, but every punch was a fair one. Schmeling fell to the canvas in just two minutes and four seconds.

Joe was such a gentleman that night of the wrestling show. He was a real class act, and that is something I really respect. Respect is always a two-way street. Before my match with Morales, I had a talk with Joe. I told him if an opportunity presented itself during the match, we'd be happy to make him look good and take some of the spotlight. Joe's reply was to the point and very simple. He said thank you, but I have had my day in the sun. He said he was at MSG to help the two of us and that he hoped we had a great show.

I knew at that moment Joe Louis was a man of respect. I had an opportunity to spend more time with him that week. We drove to Portland, Maine, together. What a great experience.

Sleeping on the Job

I loved the extra money that wrestling brought in, but I hated the routine. During the school year I was up at 6:30 AM and at the school by 8:00. I would teach a full day, usually eight hours including lunch. Then I would coach football, wrestling, or track for a few more hours. Then I would drive to the Eddystone Hotel in Detroit to catch a ride with some other wrestlers, or jump in my car and drive like heck to meet some of the boys on the road. After my first month I was always the main event, so I was last to wrestle each night. I'd jump back in the car to drive home, then got to bed around 2:00 AM. Do the math: I was getting five hours of sleep, if I was lucky. I was booked every night except Sundays and game nights. Pat, where is the Maxwell House coffee?

Saturdays were the worst, especially after Friday night football games and the parties that followed. We had three TV shows plus a house show every Saturday. Detroit TV in the morning, Grand Rapids TV at noon, then Jackson TV at 5:00 PM, and a live event each Saturday night.

While the schedule was brutal, I was soon making more money wrestling than teaching. The quality of life for my family was much better. Still, I hated being away from Pat and the kids, and I still regret that to this day. You cannot replace that lost time.

Leaping Larry Chene was one of the top performers with whom I had the pleasure of being in the ring. Larry had unbelievable ring presence and timing. Ricky Cortez was another great worker. A fellow Detroiter, Ricky had a day job at one of the factories. He also had a sleeping disorder, which he acquired during the Korean War. He could never go on the road because he would fall asleep and miss his flights. Early in my career as the Student, I was working a tag team match with Ricky as my partner. We were working against Larry and Gino Brito. It was a main event and the crowd was into the match. The Student had gotten super heat on Gino. Gino gave Larry a hot tag and I bumped big time for him. When the Student went to give Ricky the tag, Ricky was holding onto the tag team rope...sound asleep. I swear on a handful of NoDoz, that is a true story. When the Student finally woke Ricky up, he went in and promptly regained the heat. The fans thought Ricky was just being a coward when he refused my first tag. It just goes to show that Ricky could get heat even in his sleep.

Taylor Made for Wrestling

I met a young man at the high school wrestling championships in Sturgis, Michigan, one year. He was from Dowagiac, and he cornered me. He said his name was Chris Taylor and that he had graduated from high school the previous year. He asked what he had to do to become a pro wrestler. Now, I had been asked that question a lot over the years. If I had a nickel for every time I was asked that, it would not be called Trump Tower. It would be the Animal Tower.

My answer always depended upon the circumstances. Since Chris was so young, I told him he should go to college so he would have something to fall back on. Making it big in wrestling has always been akin to making the major leagues in baseball or having teeming throngs scream and shout for you as you play the electric guitar in front of a sold-out crowd at the Joe Louis Arena in Detroit or Madison Square Garden in New York City. The odds are long indeed.

Chris replied that he had gotten terrible grades in high school and could not get into college. Now that sounded familiar. Still, I was convinced that college was necessary for success. I suggested Chris look into attending either Grand Rapids Junior College or Muskegon Community College. Both had wrestling programs.

Chris went to Muskegon CC. From there, he attended Iowa State University, where he won the NCAA heavyweight championship in 1972 by defeating Greg Wojciechowski of the University of Toledo. Wojchiechowski went on to wrestle professionally as the Great Wojo. Chris also won the bronze medal at the 1972 Olympics, losing his only match to Alexander Medved.

Chris did go on to wrestle professionally. He was booked at Detroit's Cobo Arena on a card that I was also on in 1977. I can tell you that because of my high school coaching background, I was really excited for the opportunity to meet him. I had totally forgotten we had met years earlier.

I went over to Chris in the locker room and as I put my hand out to introduce myself, Chris asked, "Coach Myers, don't you remember me? I have wanted to thank you for a long, long time." He reminded me of our first meeting, and how I had advised him to go to college. He could not thank me enough.

Sadly, health problems soon forced him to retire from the ring. He died of cardiovascular complications two years later at the age of 29. God bless you, Chris.

Huddling Up in B Minor

I had a football scholarship at Michigan State but never played a down. A combination of bad grades and bad behavior sidelined me in East Lansing. But after graduation, I had an opportunity to play minor league football for the Grand Rapids Blazers of the Continental Football League (CFL). The league had a reputation as being a pretty tough place to loiter. Still, I jumped at the chance because I wanted to show people I could actually play the game. I made $100 per game while most others pulled in $50. Gary Moeller, who would later become the head coach at the University of Michigan, played right behind me at linebacker.

We'd cut up boxes and use them as arm pads. Guys would also put them around their ankles and use them for leg whips. That would be illegal now, but it wasn't then. Our coach was Jack Morton, who had been the defensive coordinator for the Green Bay Packers. He left Green Bay the year before Vince Lombardi became the Packers' coach.

We played teams in Chicago, Canton, Columbus, Louisville, and Montreal. I'd drive to Grand Rapids, and then we would fly out of there for our games. We'd get back Sunday night, and then I would drive home and teach and coach Monday morning. Back then, the CFL and the American Football League were on a similar level. They had more money, but I think we had better players. I had a chance to play with the Buffalo Bills after playing in the CFL and would have made $8,500. (By contrast, Artie Donovan of the Baltimore Colts was making $6,000.)

I also played a few games with the Portland Lions in 1959, another semipro team. In 1964, after I had started teaching, coaching, and wrestling as the Student, my path with the Lions crossed again. The

Pontiac VFW sponsored wrestling shows at the city's armory and the local wrestling promoter also handled the Pontiac Firebirds semipro football team. At one of the wrestling shows we started talking football, and the Portland team came up. When I told him I'd played for the Portland Lions, he came up with this crazy idea that the Student should suit up and play for the Firebirds when the Lions came to town.

I felt like an idiot getting dressed in football gear while also wearing the mask. None of the other players on the Firebirds had a clue who I was. While I knew most of them, I was nothing but a masked man to them.

When the game started, I was pumped. The trouble was, the mask left me with no peripheral vision. I played like a wild man, pinballing this way and that way; bumping into people like I was in a mosh pit at a rock concert. I had a ball. I was in on most of the tackles in the first half. I was calling the Portland players by name and they were screaming "Who are you?" I did not go out for the second half; I was gassed. But the mission had been accomplished. The game sold out, and so did the wrestling show the following week.

An Angel in Arms

Angels aren't always outfitted in wings. Sometimes they wear shoulder pads and sport five o'clock shadows. I did not realize when I lined up against Cowboy Bill Watts while playing football for the Grand Rapids Blazers that he was a divine presence. In fact, I thought he was a jerk. No offense, God.

We were playing in Indianapolis. The guard I was covering gave me a false read. As I stepped to my left, their tackle blocked down on me. He got such a good hit on me that he could have pushed me westbound on I-94 all the way to Chicago.

When that play was over, this jerk looked down at my feet and said, "I thought you had roller skates on."

Not exactly angelic, right? It sounded to me more like a declaration of war. We beat each other into Quaker Oats the rest of the game. I did a number on him, and I will admit this idiot came right back at me. We had a real standoff. After the game I grabbed a program to find out who the jerk was, just in case our paths crossed down the road.

Years later, our paths did indeed cross, and it was in the WWE. The jerk's name was Bill Watts, a former football player at the University of Oklahoma and a longtime wrestling champion.

Vince McMahon made a tepid attempt to keep the wrestling from going over the deep end by bringing in Cowboy Bill Watts. He turned control over to Bill, and Bill really did make a huge difference in the direction the company went for the next few months. While I really liked what Bill was trying to do, Vince could not stand watching someone else run his business. Bill Watts did not come to the WWE to be just another yes man for Vince, and when he departed the WWE three months later, it ceased being a wrestling business, in my opinion.

From the time I started in wrestling, I knew about Cowboy Bill Watts. We spent more than 30 years in the same business but had never met. Bill knew me in wrestling as George Steele. As it turned out, he had checked the Grand Rapids Blazers roster after that game years ago and saw number 69 was Jim Myers of Michigan State University. He never realized that I was also George "the Animal" Steele.

When we finally did meet again and I mentioned the game, Bill remembered it as the war it was. That bonded us together and we became very close friends.

Here's where the angel angle comes in. Cowboy Bill Watts heard I had gotten very sick and he called me. He was involved in a company that sold natural health supplements and convinced me to try them. Lo and behold, I started to get better. Was it Cowboy Bill Watts' product? Was it the prayers? Was it a change in diet? Most likely, it was a combination plate of all of the above, and mostly God reacquainting me with an angel whose early manifestations were definitely jerk-like. Maybe the Hollywood version of angels is all wrong anyway. I found God. And I found Cowboy Bill Watts, who had also found God. So what if the angel also needs shaving cream and a Bic razor?

A Sad Leap of Faith

One of the truly great wrestling performers, Leaping Larry Chene, was killed in an auto accident in Ottawa, Illinois, on October 1, 1964. He was driving to the Twin Cities to take part in a tag team match with Cowboy Jack Lanza, a babyface. They were scheduled to meet Larry Henning (Mr. Perfect's dad) and Harley Race, who were just beginning their tag team career together in the AWA. Larry had a large family and hated to leave home.

The Sheik and Larry broke into the wrestling business together. They were like brothers. The Sheik was in negotiations to buy the rights to promote Cobo Arena in Detroit and the rest of the territory when Larry died. The Sheik really wanted to get Larry involved at every level of the promotion.

Larry was a babyface and a truly great wrestler. His leaps often included the flying head scissors, a move during which he would wrap his legs around an opponent's neck and then flip them over. It was a very athletic move.

After Larry's death, the Sheik looked out for his family. While I do not know all of the details, I know it was done from the heart. The Sheik was really a great guy. The Sheik and his wife, Joyce, also took care of the children of family members who had died. They both had some great qualities.

That just shows you how different some guys can be outside of the ring. The Sheik character was a rich wild man from Syria. When he went into the ring, a manager unfurled a prayer rug and burned incense while he said his prayers to Allah. He used hidden pencils to rip apart the faces of his opponents. Another illegal move was the fireball he allegedly threw into the faces of foes. He did not speak on camera. Does any of this sound remotely familiar?

Heat Check

The Sheik and I used to work out in and around the same pond in Williamston, Michigan, when I was a freshman at Michigan State. When the Sheik took over Cobo Arena, I became a regular on the Detroit cards. The Sheik booked so many superstars that the Student got a great ring education.

Looking back, I was nothing more than cheap labor. My biggest payoff with Bert Ruby was $90. The most I ever got from the Sheik was $150. Early on, I knew the Sheik's promotion would never have room for the Student as a major player.

The Sheik had been working a program with Bobo Brazil that had major heat. My first match for the television show on Channel 9 in Windsor was a tag team match with Gary Hart. It was wild. The Student did a number on his opponent and I threw him over the ropes. After Gary also did a number on the poor guy, he tossed him back over the ropes to me.

The fans started starting chanting, "We want Bobo! We want Bobo!" The louder the fans got, the more excited Gary and I got. We thought we were really getting over, but after the match, the Sheik was livid. He wanted us to go out the next hour and have that same opponent pin the Student. I told him no.

I learned a great lesson on that TV show. The business is not about heat, it is about leverage. Wrestling was no more than a great part-time job for me.

Hall of Fame

I first met Tony Vellano in 1999 at an independent show in Troy, New York. We hit it off immediately and I believed right away that Tony was a man of integrity. After the show, we went out for a few drinks and started chatting.

Tony was very active with the Boxing Hall of Fame board and he asked me about a WWF Hall of Fame. I told him one really did not exist. There had been four inductions, and then it all came to a screeching halt.

Tony was a member of the New York State Athletic Commission. The more we talked, the more questions Tony had. He finally said that he believed professional wrestlers needed to be remembered in a brick-and-mortar Hall of Fame. All the while, we kept sipping our Scotch.

To be honest, that first conversation was just bar talk. It served mainly to fill the gaps between ordering drinks. Never in my wildest dreams did I believe our discussion would turn into reality.

About four months later, I got a call from Tony. "Tony who?" was my response. I really did not remember who he was or what he was talking about. I think it was a combination of Dewar's and dyslexia. Tony slowed down and got me up to speed. He had worked hard to get things in order to open a wrestling Hall of Fame and museum in the state of New York.

So Tony Vellano and Jim Myers became the founding fathers of the Professional Wrestling Hall of Fame. Tony quickly assembled a board of directors, made up primarily of local businessmen. We hammered out a constitution, albeit not as impressive as the one signed by George Washington and Alexander Hamilton. Something about an X from George "the Animal" Steele on the signature line takes the historic significance away from any document.

Tony did all the organizing and groundwork, while I added my name to raise visibility and to gain the respect of the wrestling community.

The next task was finding a site for the museum. Once again, after some time, Tony called and he was really excited. He had found a building in Schenectady, New York. I asked Tony for the address; remember, he did not have a clue when it came to the wrestling business. He said the building was at 123 Broadway. I nearly hit the floor—in wrestling terminology, 123 refers to a pin, and Broadway means a draw or the time limit. Talk about fate.

Two years later, we inducted our first class into the PWHF. The categories were Midgets, Ladies, Tag Teams, Pioneer Era, Television Era, and Modern Era. I had solicited nominees from 35 wrestling historians from around the country. They were the same people who voted.

The first PWHF induction was held in 2002 in Schenectady. Members of that first class were Andre the Giant, Mildred Burke, Gorgeous George, Frank Gotch, George Hackenschmidt, Ed "Strangler" Lewis, Jim Londos, Buddy Rogers, Bruno Sammartino, Sky Low Low, Ricky Steamboat, Joe Stetcher, and Lou Thesz.

Many more greats have since been inducted. Some of the not-so-greats have also sneaked in, too, including yours truly. I was a member of the class of 2005.

The Professional Wrestling Hall of Fame and Museum is now located in Amsterdam, New York. Our mission statement is to "maintain organized volunteerism that preserves and promotes the dignified history of professional wrestling. Our purpose is to enshrine and pay tribute to professional wrestlers who have advanced this national pastime in terms of athletics and entertainment. We will remain steadfast in our efforts and energies to secure and enhance the structure of our Museum, and generate community and commerce building events for betterment of the Professional Wrestling Hall of Fame and the area that is its home. In doing so we will acquire and maintain records, memorabilia, and artifacts related to professional wrestling. These enterprises will advance the legacy of the sport of professional wrestling, and give due credit and commemoration to those who have contributed to its greatness."

I feel good about my role, because it has been my way of returning something to the sport and the people who have meant so much to me all of these years.

The 1984 World Series

Most Detroit baseball fans with any rings around their trunks will remember that Kirk Gibson smacked that famous three-run homer into the upper deck in right field at Tiger Stadium to clinch the World Series against the San Diego Padres in 1984.

Prior to that home run, fans will recall Padres manager Dick Williams going to the mound to talk to relief pitcher Goose Gossage, seemingly with the intent of walking Gibson, who had already homered once that game.

Gossage, however, talked his manager out of that strategy and pitched to Gibson, who promptly smashed the ball into the seats to give the Tigers a four-run lead.

Detroit shortstop Alan Trammell won the *Sport* magazine variation of the World Series' Most Valuable Player award. What most folks don't know is that George "the Animal" Steele also played a big part in the Tigers beating the Padres.

The night before the clinching game, I took two cases of Stroh's, our local beer, along with my coaching staff from Madison High to Cobo Arena. The WWF was in town and I was taking the beer for my friends who were wrestling that night. The first wrestler I saw was Dick Murdoch, and I told Dick that I had some beer for the boys. He told me that Dick Williams was upstairs in the VIP room, along with the rest of the Padres coaching staff, and asked if I would take the beer there. There we were, partying with the Padres manager and his staff until the show ended.

Since everyone was in a pretty good mood, thanks to our sparkling personalities and the Stroh's, I invited Dick and his coaches out on the town. We went to Greektown, enjoyed some great food, and later visited some after-hours clubs. Sometime during the night, the Padres pitching coach asked me if wrestling was fake, and I thought Dick was going to fire him on the spot. Dick was a real class act and very respectful.

The robins were bathing and the sun was wiping the sleep out of its eyes when we parted ways. Before that, I gave him my phone number and he said he was going to leave his tickets at the will call window for my family. His wife was in town, but she was worried the Detroit fans would go wild if the Tigers clinched the Series that night, and her concern proved to be well founded. After the game, cars were overturned, some were torched, and it was a pretty wild scene outside of Tiger Stadium. At least the rioters wore smiles.

Can you believe I never got a World Series ring for my contribution to that championship? Dick Williams and his staff should have known better. You can't run with the big dogs...or George "the Animal" Steele.

Baseball, Part Deux

I was on my way to a football clinic at the University of Michigan with my high school staff one Friday. On the way, we stopped at the Southfield Marriott for a bite to eat. Right in front of the hotel, a crowd had gathered. Right away, I realized it was a sports team of some sort. I asked the waiter who they were and was told it was the Texas Rangers.

Bruce Pettibone, who was on my coaching staff, was also the baseball coach at the high school. He had played second base at Michigan State and was a huge baseball fan. Bruce said he wanted to go back to the car, get his clipboard, and then ask the Rangers players for some autographs. I grabbed him by his arm and told him to that he was never to ask for autographs when he was with me.

Maybe three minutes later, Sparky Lyle of the Rangers recognized me. Well, it'd be more accurate to say he recognized George "the Animal" Steele. Sparky and the other players with him went nuts. Their afternoon game against the Tigers had been rained out, and the downtown area was not the safest place to hang around in those days. Sparky was carrying on with some gal whose face would've made a pit bull tuck its tail between its legs and run. He said, "Look at this ugly gal.

I would not give her the time of day in New York, but this is Detroit!"
Everybody laughed.

Rangers manager Pat Corrales was in the bar and told me that their
trainer was a huge wrestling fan and he was going to give him a call. Bill
Ziegler came downstairs carrying a program from a wrestling show at
New York's Madison Square Garden, and I was on the cover. We all had
a great time, but my staff and I ended up a little late for the football clinic
in Ann Arbor.

CHAPTER 12

From Ring Ropes to Velvet Ropes

When Pat and I go to the movies, we buy our tickets just like everyone else. We grumble about paying $10 each for flicks that sometimes don't even kick back a couple of bucks' worth of entertainment. We fork over an eye-popping $5 for a box of Jujubes or a small bag of Twizzlers, and swallow our pride to shell out $7 for about 55 cents' worth of popcorn.

That is why my role in Tim Burton's 1994 film *Ed Wood* was such a departure, albeit a temporary one.

The movie starred Johnny Depp as cult filmmaker Ed Wood. It dealt with Wood's relationship with Bela Lugosi, who was played by Martin Landau. Among the others in the cast were Sarah Jessica Parker, Patricia Arquette, Jeffrey Jones, and Bill Murray.

Oh yeah, and me; I played Tor Johnson. Now, out of all those names, who does not belong on the marquee of your local movie theater? For once, at the world premiere in New York City, the Sno-Caps were free and so were the cups of soda pop (even if there was still a little bit too much ice).

When Tim called me about possibly being in the movie, Pat and I were home in Cocoa Beach. I thought it was a rib. I was sure another wrestler was playing a practical joke on me. I had been in a lot of productions, both as a wrestler and then as an agent for the WWF, but in a movie? With real movie stars? Right, and Brad Pitt is about to dump Angelina Jolie for Honey Boo Boo's mom.

Tim called because he said I looked like the late Tor Johnson, a Swedish wrestler who had been in a few of Ed Wood's movies. I was flattered; I never figured I looked like a movie star. That flattered feeling lasted about 10 seconds; that's how long it took me to find out that Tor Johnson, a massive man who stood about 6'5", had played the monster in some of Wood's productions—without benefit of makeup.

Edward Davis "Ed" Wood, Jr. was a screenwriter, director, producer, actor, author, and film editor of rather dubious talent. In the 1950s he made a number of low-budget genre films. In the '60s and '70s he made pornographic movies and wrote pulp crime, horror, and sex novels. In 1980, he was posthumously awarded a Golden Turkey Award as the worst director of all time.

Still, the publication of Rudolph Grey's biography *Nightmare of Ecstasy: The Life and Art of Edward D. Wood, Jr.* in 1992 led to Burton's film. It would become a critically acclaimed movie and earn two Academy Awards.

Before I got involved in the movie, I did not know anything about Ed Wood, and very little at all about Tim Burton. While I had never seen *Plan 9 From Outer Space*, people had told me that they'd seen me in this monster movie. I had no clue at the time what they were talking about. Later on, I learned it was an Ed Wood movie featuring Tor Johnson. Apparently Tim Burton was not the only one who saw some resemblance between me and ol' Tor.

After I got the call from Tim, he sent me the script and asked me to send him back a video. I shot this crazy skit with Harvey Wippleman and a wrestler Harvey was managing, a nearly 8-foot-tall guy named Giant Gonzales. We filmed it at one of the WWF TV shoots. I naively sent this crazy production to one of the biggest directors in Hollywood. Tim sent the video back with a note that said while the skit was very entertaining, he'd prefer I just read a few lines from the script and send that to him. Still, I think that skit got Tim's attention.

The second audition was just as crazy. Pat and I went out and rented a video camera from a store that used to be located on A1A in Florida. The store is long gone now, just like my movie career. I swear on a stack of Cecil B. DeMille's films, we did not even know how to load the video cartridge into the camera. Pat was the cinematographer, the producer, and the director. I delivered my lines looking straight into the camera, and Pat's distended voice came from the north 40. We shot the entire video in our condo in Cocoa Beach, and I am sure it was the worst thing that Tim Burton had ever seen in his life. We really did not have any idea what he wanted. It was like Jane Goodall trying to film the chimps, only I was the one picking ticks off my hairy chest, with a hankering from some bananas.

Tim then said he wanted to meet with me. We got together in his office. It was the strangest place I'd ever been in—and remember, being in professional wrestling I had occupied and visited a lot of out-of-the-ordinary locales. There were stuffed bats hanging all over the place. There was a replica of Edward Scissorhands. The office was painted black and he fit right into the color scheme. He was dressed all in black and had long, stringy black hair.

Tim and I sat down and had a conversation. He told me that he was looking for somebody who resembled Tor Johnson and said I definitely had the face for it but might not be tall enough. He said we might be able to compensate by using different camera angles or prosthetics in my shoes.

Two months later, Tim called and told me I had the part. Truthfully, I did look an awful lot like Tor Johnson. We were both something of a cross between Rock Hudson and Uncle Fester from *The Addams Family*. When Pat heard the news she was very excited. Hollywood, here we come! Could free popcorn and soda be far behind?

As soon as I got to California, I was told to spend time with a dialect coach. She was Swedish, which was Tor Johnson's nationality. Pat arrived a month later and they put us both up in a nice, corporate apartment. We lived there for a few months. We were on the top floor, but when Pat first arrived, she accidentally went into an apartment on the first floor. There were already a bunch of suitcases on the floor and five people of Asian descent were staring at her as she walked through the door.

We shot the movie all over Los Angeles, using sites Ed Wood actually used in his own movies. Tim Burton wanted to recreate scenes exactly the way they had been done originally.

Everybody on the set was great to me. Sarah Jessica Parker was a little more reserved than everyone else, but that might have been because she arrived on the set later than the rest of us. I remember she carried a little dog around with her.

Bill Murray is both a great guy and a great actor. He first gained national exposure on *Saturday Night Live*, which earned him an Emmy Award. He was nominated for an Academy Award for *Lost in Translation*. His other movies have included *Caddyshack*, *Ghostbusters*, *Rushmore*, and *Moonrise Kingdom*.

Martin Landau was also a very nice man. He began his acting career in the 1950s, and his early films included a supporting role in Alfred Hitchcock's *North by Northwest*. His role as Bela Lugosi in *Ed Wood* earned him an Academy Award, a Screen Actors Guild Award, and a Golden Globe.

Johnny Depp was also great. He became a teen idol on the 1980s television series *21 Jump Street*. He's been in movies such as *Edward*

Scissorhands, Charlie and the Chocolate Factory, and the *Pirates of the Caribbean* franchise. His films have grossed more than $7.6 billion worldwide. He has been nominated for Best Actor at the Academy Awards three times and twice been named Sexiest Man Alive by *People* magazine.

Patricia Arquette has also appeared in films such as *True Romance, Lost Highway, Stigmata, Holes,* and *A Nightmare on Elm Street 3.* She played the lead character in the television series *Medium,* for which she received an Emmy.

Surprisingly, I have never been nominated for an Emmy, a Golden Globe, an Academy Award, or even a Sexiest Man Alive award. Who said voter fraud is limited to dangling chads in Florida?

I was not nervous at all on the day I showed up to shoot my first scene. I think most of the actors and actresses figured I would be petrified, but as Bill Murray said to me, "You've been acting for years, so you shouldn't be nervous."

That was true. While professional wrestling is not fake in terms of the toll it takes on the body, George "the Animal" Steele was not who I really was. All that maniacal behavior was the stuff of Hollywood—or at least McMahon—whether we were in New York City, Boston, Pittsburgh, Detroit, or Tokyo. We played to full houses in places like Madison Square Garden, the Boston Garden, and the Pontiac Silverdome. Acting was in my blood, in a way.

Props were a part of both endeavors. When I was the Student, my first mask consisted of a woman's girdle with strategic holes cut into it. I hardly ever left the locker room without my secret weapon. When I played Tor Johnson, I wore white contact lenses with tiny pinholes in them so I could see. In one of the scenes, we were in a dark movie theater and I could barely see at all. I was tripping all over the place and the other actors helped me out. After all, we weren't supposed to be shooting *The Miracle Worker* or *Wait Until Dark.* The platform shoes I wore probably did not help my mobility, either.

The entire experience was very enjoyable. Pat and I had a great time. We went to the premiere in New York City at the Lincoln Center. I guess premieres are usually about actors sucking up to the media and interviews stiffer than heavily starched collars, but this one was different. It was more like a family wedding; it was one big party. Sure, the press was in attendance, but everybody was eating and drinking and dancing.

I had to laugh, though. When we first went out to California to do the movie, I told Pat we shouldn't get caught up in all the excitement. But guess what I was doing after two months in Hollywood? I started looking for an agent! A couple of them told me that if I moved to California, I could get steady work in the movies because of the way I looked. But I was not about to move to California. None of my family lived there. My brother, Jack, and his family still lived in Michigan. Also, I was still pretty sick. If you watch the film, you can see that my face is very swollen from all the Prednisone I was taking to combat my Crohn's disease.

Despite that, we both had a great experience on *Ed Wood*. How many people get an opportunity to jump into the Hollywood lifestyle for a few months and then get back to reality?

My only regret is that when we go to the movies now, Pat wants to stay to the very end of the credits to see if we know any of the people involved in the movie.

Well, I guess there is one more regret: we have to pay for popcorn and soda pop these days, too.

CHAPTER 13

A Family Affair

On Take Your Sons and Daughters to Work Day, the kids go with you to the office. They spend time looking at your cubicle. Geez, that's exciting. Where'd you get that nice Sierra Club calendar, Dad? How about that Shaq bobblehead? Or maybe you work on the loading dock. The kids total 90 minutes on the job—45 minutes spent looking around the warehouse dodging forklifts and 45 more staring into empty 18-wheelers.

When the Myers kids went with me to work in the summer, it was a little bit more exciting for them. My office was Madison Square Garden, the Boston Garden, or any number of arenas along the East Coast. Our roster at home numbered three. Pat and I had Felicia in 1955. Randy was born in 1960, and Dennis came along two years after his brother. All three of our kids are now married and have children.

As Randy remembers, "We'd go for four or five weeks at a time. Usually it would be up and down the East Coast following Dad's matches. It was pretty exciting to be an insider. A lot of times we would go in the locker room. Some of the guys we always saw were Andre the Giant, Chief Jay Strongbow, and Pedro Morales."

Randy and his wife, Kim, have three children: 24-year-old Will, 22-year-old Ryan, and 21-year-old Brett.

"My recollection is Dad was gone most of the summer," said Randy, now an executive with Jabbil, an international company specializing in product solutions for electronics and technology companies. "Dad would come back home periodically during the summer, but he would be away for much of it. Catching up with Dad while he was wrestling was our summer vacation. It would be driving up and down the East Coast, primarily.

"That is the way we grew up. We would go to Dad's shows. I remember going in the back way to arenas. We could hang out with the other wrestlers sometimes. This was when we were younger and it was pre-WWF/WWE. It was cool. I enjoyed it."

Dennis; his wife, Cindi; and their five children reside in northern Michigan. He is in the mortgage business.

"As a kid, all my friends would be excited when they found out my dad was a wrestler," said Dennis. "To us, it was just the norm. It was part of life. In hindsight, it made for great travel and even greater memories. We were able to spend a lot of time together and do things you could not do if your mom or dad or both were normal working people.

"There were a couple of years when we rented places in New Jersey, and that was our home base for the summer. Since I have a summer birthday, I would always have my birthday in a hotel room and that was neat. We'd either have a pool or a beach and that was great.

"My brother and I did quite a bit together. We'd go with my dad to the shows frequently. We would get to wrestle in the ring prior to anyone else being there. We would help set the ring up. We'd go in the locker room and sometimes watch the shows from there. Wrestlers I really remember seeing a lot were Bruno Sammartino, Pedro Morales, Chief Jay Strongbow, Mr. Fuji, and Tanaka. We would walk through the corridors and people would be staring at us. They would wonder who those kids were. It was kind of wild."

While Randy and Dennis loved the shows and all the trappings of wrestling, there was not much laughter when Felicia first started going to those shows. I was still using the Student character at that time, and much like George "the Animal" Steele for most of my career, he was reviled, a certifiable heel. The crowd shouted things that were mostly R-rated. Their comments were not the stuff of Disney or Pixar—or even truck drivers stuck in rush-hour traffic.

"I used to end up in the bathroom almost all of the time, crying," said Felicia, who now teaches at Western Michigan University. "Dad was a bad guy and people were always screaming obscenities at him. They'd tell him to go to hell and call him a son of a bitch. People absolutely hated him. They threw popcorn at him. They doused him with glasses of soda. I just did not like going, and when I got old enough, I did not go. We'd rent a house near Atlantic City and when I was a teenager, I would just stay on the beach.

"I remember once my grandmother went with us to a show at Cobo Hall in Detroit. A woman who held an umbrella over her head was screaming all sorts of profanities at my dad. She was sitting right in front of us and my grandmother leaned over and asked, 'Do you realize that man has a mother somewhere?' While my grandmother never said she was Dad's mom, the woman in front of us put her umbrella down and was quiet for the rest of the show."

Those memories are funny now, but for years, Felicia had nightmares about me getting hurt in the ring. They lasted even into her first year or two of college at Central Michigan University. In particular, she disliked the blood. Felicia would always ask me before matches if I would get cut that night. If I said yes, she would not even watch.

Over the years, Take Your Sons and Daughters to Work Day evolved. I got older and so did our kids. When Felicia's daughter, Melissa, was in the first grade, her school had a Grandparents Day. At that time, George "the Animal" Steele was at the height of his popularity. I had become a loveable cartoon character, adored by millions. What could be more welcoming than a grade-school classroom?

"Everybody loved Melissa's grandpa," said Felicia. "Everyone wanted to spend time with him. The other students were hugging him, the teachers wanted autographs, the principal wanted an autograph. Melissa came home from school crying, saying, 'Mom, I wish I had a grandpa like everyone else, then I could have spent time with him.' The next day, there was a front-page story in the local paper about George 'the Animal' Steele being in town."

While Felicia was the first-born and did not play high school sports, the perspective of our boys was unique. I was their dad. I was also on the pro wrestling circuit. I was also a teacher and a coach. So, Dad was their father and an intimidating coach for them and many, many others. The fear factor was not just something limited to the wrestling ring.

"I was in the seventh grade when we moved from Royal Oak to Madison Heights," said Dennis. "Being the new kid, I wanted to meet other kids and make friends. Usually dad could keep his lives separate. George 'the Animal' Steele was one guy; the teacher and coach was another guy; and my dad was yet another guy. He was able to draw the line when it needed to be drawn."

"But that was not always the case. When I would bring people over to the house for the first time, Dad would go into his George 'the Animal' Steele routine and chase them. They would pee their pants and they would run out of the house frightened to death. It was not easy making new friends at first."

But that act only went so far, especially at home. Dennis recalls being on the wrong end of a couple of spankings when he was younger, and that was all it took for Dad to make a lasting impression. But once when he was 10 or 11 years old, Dennis recalls irritating his mother to the point where she issued every mother's ultimate warning: "Wait until your father gets home!"

"I do not remember what I had done," said Dennis. "When Dad got home, he took me immediately into the bedroom, slammed the door, and then quietly told me that he was not going to hit me with the belt. He was going to smack the bed with it. He also said I should scream loudly after every smack, and after a minute or so run directly into my room and act like I was crying. So that's what I did."

George "the Animal" Steele, wrestling's renowned heel for years and years, with a soft, Hallmark-card side? The same guy who punched opponents, rendered them ineffective with his flying hammerlock, and generally turned them into quivering puddles of protoplasm? Despite what Dennis said, I plead the fifth.

We had moved to a house right across the street from the football field the summer before Randy started high school. Randy was the captain of both the football and wrestling teams when he was a senior at Madison High School.

"We did that not so much because Dad wanted to coach me. My recollection is, if we did not move I think Mom and Dad figured he would never see me or Dennis. I mean, we would have been playing all of those sports at another high school [Royal Oak Dondero] and Dad would have been coaching at Madison High School at the same time," said Randy.

While Randy was a very good all-around athlete, he prefers to describe himself as a "mediocre quarterback" and a "pretty good wrestler." He played on the varsity football team for three years, and was the quarterback as a junior and senior. He started his high school wrestling career at 126 pounds and topped out at 145.

"When Dad was home from professional wrestling, he was pretty much coaching all of the time. He did football and basketball and even track for a short time. Before I got to high school, I had already watched him coach for years. When we were younger, Mom would drop us off at one of his practices. That is how we spent a lot of time, either watching practices or going to games. Because I had watched Dad coaching for so long, I got an appreciation for him and what he did," Rudy said.

"He was a tough coach. He certainly had an intimidating way about him. I was a decent athlete, but nothing great. I do remember Dad not taking it all home with him. He was able to separate family life from athletics.

"Probably the best story about wrestling was when I was a junior and it was the consolation semifinals at the state meet. The kid who was supposed to win the state championship had just gotten [beaten], so he had fallen to the losers' bracket and he was my opponent. It was a great match and it was close. I think I was up by a point or two, and while I can't remember the circumstances, all of a sudden he slapped the heck out of me. I think he was mad because of his previous match. When he did that, my dad jumped up and started to come onto the mat. I just turned to Dad and told him that I'd handle it. I proceeded to kick the kid's butt pretty well after that. From then on, I think Dad realized I did not need his protection anymore. Dad always points to that as the moment when my maturity really showed up."

I had to exhibit some maturity of my own when my undefeated Madison Eagles football team went to nearby Clawson to conclude the regular season. Most everyone expected Madison to go into the playoffs with a clean slate, but that's not what happened. The team Randy was on lost to a Clawson team that still finished below .500 and knocked us out of a chance at the playoffs, but I kept my cool. I told everyone they had an outstanding season, and not to put their heads down. The kids needed that kind of talk.

Dennis needed a comforting talk himself during his senior season of wrestling. He went into the state meet as the top seed at 185 pounds, but lost his first two matches and was bounced out of the tournament.

"I was wrestling the 16th-seeded kid in my first match, and I got caught and he pinned me," Dennis said. "The next match, I was in just sort of a fog. I think I lost on points. I really do not remember. Obviously

I was crying, but my dad was very supportive. He never acted like he was upset, but as the father of five children now myself, I am sure he was dying inside.

"I went on to Central Michigan University, too, just like Randy and Felicia, and I had a chance to get a partial wrestling scholarship. I think they were going to pay for books or something, but as much as I enjoyed the sport and the meets and such, I hated practice. For two hundred dollars or whatever books cost back then, there was no way I was going to put myself through all of those practices. I just said forget it and concentrated on academics.

"I know Dad always felt guilty about leaving in the summer. He told us that. But the way I look at it was, I got to spend a lot more time with my dad than other kids did. I mean, he was also my teacher and coach. I would see him at school, and then I would see him at practice as well as games and meets. Most parents just drop their kids off at school or practices and just leave. Dad was always there.

"One of my favorite memories was when I went to a Michigan State football game with Randy and my dad. We stayed in a hotel room at the Kellogg Center. Dad picked up a case of beer after the game. I was probably 21 and Randy was 23. That's when I realized my dad was also a just a big kid. He told us all of his war stories of high school and college, and he probably did worse stuff then I did. I respected him for telling us all of that stuff."

Dennis also played football for me. He was a cornerback as a sophomore, and a quarterback his junior and senior seasons. It was Dennis who got revenge for Randy's upset loss against Clawson. The tables had been turned, and it was winless Madison taking on undefeated Clawson. We knocked Clawson out of the playoffs by beating them.

The tables turned at the Myers house, whether it was in Royal Oak or Madison Heights. While George "the Animal" Steele presented the image of intimidation, it was actually Pat who ruled our household. Forget Randy Savage, Hulk Hogan, or Bruno Sammartino; it was Pat who got the pin every time.

"I don't think Dad ever even cut the grass, or if he did it had to be when we were pretty young," said Randy, laughing.

Dennis put it even more succinctly.

"Mom pretty much ruled the roost," he said. "She did everything, really. She paid the bills and kept everything in sync. Dad was gone a lot during the summer, and I remember my sister, Felicia, being the built-in babysitter."

Randy was a team captain and president of his senior class. He went on to walk-on in football at Central Michigan University for a year before he decided academics held the key to his future, not athletics. He majored in business and has been a success at it ever since.

"It was Mom who made sure, when we went to places like Washington, D.C., during the summer [that we saw] all of the monuments and things, and when we were in places like Boston, we visited all the historic sites," said Randy. "She made sure we saw some plays and things like that for some culture. It certainly wasn't Dad.

"Mom obviously played a big role in raising us. She was the planner. She was always one step ahead of everything that needed to happen. She started taking college courses when I started going to school, I think. Mom started teaching when my brother, Dennis, was old enough to go to school. She was still teaching [until] my mom and dad moved to Florida."

Pat spent about a decade teaching in the Madison schools. She spent a lot more time than that helping me keep my perspective on things. Imagine a teacher and coach like me who rode on buses suddenly segueing to limousines. A husband and father from a small town in the suburbs of Detroit who is also the object of both anger and adoration of thousands night after night in wrestling arenas. It was quite a transition every summer. Jim Myers, meet Pat Myers. Pat had a way of knowing how to tell George "the Animal" Steele to check his ego at the door.

"When Jim would come from a summer of wrestling, it was back to life with his wife and kids," she said. "The transition took a little while. His brain was still out east, where everybody waited on him. I'd have to tell him not to throw wet towels on the floor and to turn off the lights when he left a room. I'd literally tell him to put George back in the box. The Junkyard Dog's wife and I talked about it. We'd say they suffer from the Motel Syndrome. It took a few weeks of teaching and coaching and dealing with parents to get over it and get [him] back to reality. I mean, he would get off the plane and almost go right to practice. It was quite a quick transition."

Sometimes Pat put things in perspective without even verbalizing it. That could happen on the road in Michigan or elsewhere.

Pat was with me in New York when a limo picked us up at the hotel. We were going to a video store in one of the boroughs for an autograph signing. When we got there, the line was wrapped around the block. I had the driver pull around back. I went inside to meet the people and sign autographs and Pat stayed in the limo. She had papers to correct for her sixth-grade class. That pretty much showed me what was important and what wasn't.

Pat was an A student in high school. She had planned on going to college and becoming a teacher right away, but didn't someone once say that life happens when you are busy making other plans? We had Felicia before we got to Michigan State, had Randy while I was a student in East Lansing, and Dennis arrived two years after that.

Both Pat and I felt it was very important for her to be at home as much as possible when the kids were young. But she always had the hankering to get her college education, and that is exactly what she did.

"College was always in the back of my mind," she said. "I wanted a college degree and I actually wanted to be an accountant first. So I started at Oakland Community College to get my associate's degree, and then Oakland University for a bachelor's degree.

"I think the teaching bug crept up on me. I'd been around Jim with his teaching and coaching and I knew it would be something I would enjoy. I had a language arts major and a math/science minor and actually did wind up teaching middle school math my last few years."

Prior to that, Pat taught the sixth grade at two schools in the Madison school district.

Going to school and raising three kids is quite a juggling act. Getting everyone to school and getting everyone's homework done, including your own, is the ultimate in multitasking. Hey, Mom, what's for dinner? Hey, Mom, I need some poster board for a school project! Hey, Mom, where are my blue jeans and my Detroit Lions T-shirt?

"If I was going to be a little bit late from school, the kids would go to a neighbor's house down the street," said Pat. "They'd only have to be there a little while until either I got home or Jim got home."

Sure, there was pot roast once in a while. There was also chicken or ham or meat loaf. But there were also the beloved TV dinners on occasion. Who among us has not devoured a Banquet pot pie or two? Toss in some tater tots and you've got the meal of kings and queens.

We did not go out to eat that often, but when we did there was a Beefcarver restaurant in Royal Oak that featured a buffet line. The Myers clan used to hit that on Friday nights before I had to get to my football games. While Pat and I kept things pretty simple, the kids usually opted for whatever they could get their hands on.

The apple did not fall far from the tree when it came to Felicia's eventual career choice. She went down to Florida and taught in Polk County, one of the most impoverished in the state.

"I was at the poorest high school in the second poorest county in the state," she said. "The kids I was teaching had no stability in their lives. A parent might have been in prison. There might not have had any hot water at home or food on the table. As a teacher, you were not as concerned about trying to make sure everyone got a 4.0, but rather figuring out how to make a student's life better. That is the part of education people forget. It is not all test scores and grades. It is about making [better people] out of young people, some of whom do not have anything.

"I know that my father has touched and changed countless lives. I can remember when I was in grade school and he had one of his football players living with us for a while. This boy was not getting along with his parents and had moved out of the house. I recall a conversation I overheard between my dad and this boy. My dad was telling him this was not a long-term solution and that he was also partly responsible for repairing his broken family. 'You can't just walk away from it,' my dad told him."

Pat and I vowed never to walk away from our responsibilities. Take Your Sons and Daughters to Work Day? More important, take your kids home day after day and love them. Love them after they leave the house, too.

CHAPTER 14

A Deathly Pall in the Sunshine State

The doctors diagnosis was Crohn's disease. They told me I was going to die and recommended Pat and I move to the Alps to spend my last days. The problem was, with my bum knees, the last thing I was into was mountain climbing. I am not a big fan of yodeling or Swiss Miss Pudding either. I enjoy sun-splashed beaches much more than snow-capped peaks, so Pat and I opted for Florida instead.

Luckily, the doctor was wrong. More than two decades later, no funeral arrangements have yet been made.

I had left teaching and coaching in 1986 to devote myself to wrestling full-time. The money had just gotten too big to leave it in the rearview mirror every fall. Vince McMahon had a masterful touch when it came to business. He was like Midas with some hair gel (or was that Aqua Net?). Everything he touched turned to gold.

Business in 1986 was phenomenal. We were turning into rock stars (even though seeing me with an electric guitar trying to wedge myself into some of those tight leather pants would've been a sight to behold, wouldn't it?). Forget the ham sandwich; Janis Joplin could have gagged on that image alone.

Hulk Hogan was undoubtedly the biggest rock star of all of us. He was a walking, talking, flexing, shirt-ripping corporation. He was Mick Jagger with biceps and Paul McCartney with a bandanna. He was Bill Gates with adoring fans, Donald Trump with six-pack abs. Fans loved him. Hulk almost single-handedly led wrestling out of the carnival tent and into the mainstream. In an industry that had always been filled with larger-than-life characters, the Hulkster was the biggest character of them all.

In the 1980s, he was one of the world's most recognizable celebrities. That was the case even though there was no TMZ, no Twitter accounts, and no camera phones. He could not walk through an airport without collecting more kids than the Pied Piper with a pocketful of Gummi Bears. He could not go out to eat without drawing more stares than Pam Anderson walking nude down Rodeo Drive. If he stopped to talk or sign autographs, he'd either miss his flight or lose his limousine.

There was a lot of jealousy among some wrestlers as Hulk's fame grew, but I never shared it. While my tongue might have been green, envy did not turn me the same shade. Later on, after I had exited the ring and became an agent, I really turned into a major fan of Hulk Hogan because I had an up-close and personal perspective. At the height of his fame, he was in great demand with the Make-A-Wish Foundation, an organization which helps grant wishes to children with life-threatening medical conditions.

Extremely ill children would be brought to arenas in ambulances or other means of transportation. Some arrived on stretchers or in wheelchairs. You could tell that a lot of them did not have many more days to mark off the calendar, but when they saw the Hulkster, that was the furthest thing from their minds. Their faces would light up and their smiles were worthy of any Crest toothpaste commercial. Hulk was never anything but gracious and genuine. After posing with the kids and their families for pictures, he would take the child aside from his or her mom, dad, and other family members so they could share some private words.

I am not sure what he said to those stricken kids, but there were two incidents in particular that I witnessed that still give me chills.

The first occurred in Cleveland with a little boy that was about 11 years old. He came in on a stretcher and the doctors had given him just days to live. Hulk had hurried back from his workout to meet the little guy. The timing was perfect, as Hulk was just getting out of his limo as they were rolling the youngster over. Their eyes locked, and the little boy was beaming. The Hulkster went up to the boy and the youngster took Hulk's hands and smiled. Hulk promptly took off his still-sweaty workout gloves and put them on his newest buddy.

The youngster was so swollen from medication that he hardly moved. As Hulk leaned in close to whisper and listen, the boy reached out to touch Hulk's bandanna. Hulk promptly handed him the bandanna. Then his eyes fixed on Hulk's workout belt. Hulk smiled, shrugged, and with a twinkle in his eye, gave him the workout belt. The Hulkster might as well have been Santa Claus as far as that boy was concerned.

Six weeks later, we were back in Cleveland. The family was there to see Hulk Hogan, but their son was not with them. They had a gift for Hulk. It was a picture of the Hulk's little buddy in a small coffin. He was wearing Hulk's gloves, bandanna, and workout belt. The family and the Hulk hugged and the tears started to flow.

The second incident happened in Indianapolis. It involved a young girl who was also about 11 years old. Her dad told Hulk that his daughter had been acting very differently. He was not sure if she realized her disease was terminal or not.

Hulk and the ill child moved away from everyone but me; I was still within earshot when Hulk told her that someday they would meet again in heaven. The little girl started to cry, and she told the Hulk that yes, she was going to die soon, but no, she would not be in heaven. Hulk said she might get to heaven before he did because he had a few more bad guys to take care of, but he reassured her they would indeed meet in heaven someday. She started crying even louder and said, "Hulk, you don't understand. I can't go to heaven." When Hulk asked her why, she told her about a man at the hospital who was touching her under the covers.

It looked like the vein in Hulk's head was going to burst. If looks could kill, that guy in the hospital would have fallen stone-cold dead. Hulk reassured her that she was going to heaven, that she was not a bad girl, that she was one of God's little children.

Hulk then pulled the father aside and told him what was going on. He also told the dad that whatever he decided to do, he would have the Hulk's support in every way. With that, the family left the building. Wrestling impacted so many people in many different ways.

Little did I know that serious illness and doubts about going to heaven were two concepts that I would soon wrestle with myself.

There was nobody like Hulk Hogan, but ours was a traveling road show unlike any before seen in the industry. I was constantly hopping on planes and into limos with people such as Hulk Hogan, Randy Savage, Hillbilly Jim, Bam Bam Bigelow, Superstar Billy Graham, Jake "the Snake" Roberts, Blackjack Mulligan, Bret Hart, the Islanders, Jim Neidhart, and plenty of other folks.

It sounds glamorous, wrestling in front of packed arenas from Boston to St. Louis to Cape Canaveral to Long Island. Believe me, with the money being thrown around, nobody was really complaining. There was nothing wrong with room service and meal money and making $250,000 per year or more.

But wrestling 90 consecutive days and constant travel can wear a person down, especially a person like me, who was twice as old as a lot of the other guys. I referred to myself as a dinosaur trying to run with the young bucks.

Anyone who travels even occasionally knows that with every day on the road looms another potential problem. Maybe the alarm clock in your room opts to take the day off. Maybe the shuttle bus from the hotel to the airport is full, so you have to wait for the second shuttle that leaves 30 minutes later and by time you get to the airport, your plane from Minneapolis to Los Angeles is already crossing the Continental Divide. Maybe your luggage gets lost. Maybe your scheduled opponent is also having travel problems, so rather than appearing on a wrestling show, he's listed as MIA and is being searched for by John Walsh, the FBI, and Dog the Bounty Hunter.

Sleep might be your toughest opponent on the road. After a match, it took a while for the adrenaline to leave your system. So, you went out to dinner instead. That dinner was accompanied by a beer or two. There was always a wise guy in the joint. There are always people who would love to be your alleged friends. Either way, the alarm clock beckoned at 6:00 AM, whether your head hit the pillow at 11:00 PM or 3:00 AM.

Once the wake-up call came, it was time to hit the rewind button. Is this Boston or Baltimore or Biloxi? Is it the Bellagio in Vegas or the Hilton in Miami Beach or Trump Tower in New York City? Even glitter and gold becomes a grind after a while.

I began to feel really run down. I could barely put one foot in front of the other. I knew I needed something, and a doctor back in Michigan began giving me what I called jet fuel. It was not anything illegal, just a cocktail of vitamins and minerals which I took intravenously. That would work for four or five days, and then I would get back to the doctor. Eventually, it hardly worked at all, and I told Vince McMahon I needed to take some time off.

I went to see another doctor in Michigan. He immediately sent me to the hospital, and that became my return address for the next month. I could not eat. I could hardly drink. Everything was delivered through tubes. At first they told me I had ulcerated colitis. Then they told me I had Crohn's. Then they served up a combination plate of both.

Ultimately, the doctors decided on Crohn's, an inflammatory bowel disease that can affect everything from the mouth to the anus. The doctors flooded my system with pharmaceuticals. I was on 120 mgs of Prednisone, Flagyl 6mp, Dipentum, and Imuran. Among the side effects were drug-induced diabetes, irregular heartbeat, blood clots, cataracts, and dehydration. I was in bad, bad shape. They even blew "Taps" my way on a couple of occasions. The Animal was very nearly roadkill.

One hellacious day, I almost grabbed that bugle and played "Taps" myself. We were still living in Michigan, and Pat had gone to work. I woke up and every joint in my body screamed in agony. Now, I can handle pain pretty well; in fact, plenty of times it has had to cry uncle when I refused to acknowledge its presence. This was not one of those times. Every move I made was accompanied by searing pain. This was after months of being deathly, deathly ill. I decided enough was enough. If this was the way my life was going to be, I did not see the point of hanging around any longer. I did not want to be a burden to anyone.

I hobbled out to the garage. I grabbed a vacuum hose and stuck one end into the tailpipe of my car. I fished the other end through a window and rolled it up tight. I figured if life was going to be a living hell, I might as well make those accommodations permanent. I started the car, put a sleeping pill in my mouth, slipped a country-western cassette into the tape player, and prepared to punch out for good.

Even today, I am not sure why I did not go through with it. The only thing I can figure is that God does not just do hymns, He also enjoys some country music twang. Somehow amidst all of that physical and mental pain, God gave me the courage to turn off the ignition. Then and there, I decided that instead of welcoming death, I was going to embrace life. I had always been a goal-oriented person, going back to when my dad sat me at that damnable desk until I got my schoolwork done. My latest goal would be to beat this thing called Crohn's and get back to actually living life. I went back into the house and slept more soundly than I had for a long, long time.

The following day, I was sitting inside when I saw my mother coming up the driveway. It was a cold day in March and I did not want her to wait outside for long, so I got up quickly to open the door for her. Just as my mom reached the porch, I lost my balance and my head went through the glass door. I was bleeding and glass was everywhere. "Gee, next time I'll wear some makeup," said my mom, who was 77 years old at the time. Even though I was still shaking, I could not stop laughing.

Not long after, I went to a bookstore. It was in a little strip mall in Royal Oak, Michigan. I started looking for a book that dealt with auras, remembering that mysterious man in Pittsburgh who had somehow taken the pain away after Jack had injured his knee. I did not know where to look and I was too embarrassed to ask anyone. Auras still sounded like they should arrive with burning incense and some Ravi Shankar music. But I was curious and I started wandering around, looking first in their psychology section and then the psychiatry area. I felt a little sheepish and more than a little out of place. After all, I am still dyslexic, so me and bookstores share an uneasy truce at best. But there, near the door, I saw *Hands of Light: A Guide to Healing Through the Human Energy Field*. On the cover was a bluish hand with electricity coming out of the fingers. I figured it was a book on massage or something. I kept looking, but for some reason, I was still drawn to *Hands of Light*. It *was* all about auras, along with visualization and healing. It was really in-depth stuff, but I figured I had nothing to lose. I was dying and traditional medicines were not helping me. I truly believe that God led me to that bookstore.

In her book, Barbara Brennan presents an in-depth study of auras, the human energy field which we all possess. An aura, according to Brennan, impacts happiness, health, and a person's ability to reach his or her full potential.

While I was no longer really worried about realizing my full potential, the health and happiness aspects piqued my interest. I wanted to be healthy enough to keep breathing; that would certainly make me happy.

While God might have led me to that bookstore, He never said He was going to make things easy. The yellow brick road has not been without potholes. Not long after, I shut down again in Florida. I was still on heavy-duty Prednisone, which can bring on diabetes. I had a severe drop in my blood sugar level and I went into a coma. At the time I was in the shower and I did not have any idea what was going on. I fell, wedged between the tub and the toilet. Pat called 911 and a tiny blonde who was all of 90 pounds was the first to arrive. She could not have physically gotten me out of my predicament herself. She would've needed a front end loader and the jaws of life. Finally, two or three larger people showed up and they were able to extricate me from the bathroom. They put me on a gurney, and I heard one of them shout, "We're losing him!" The heart monitor flatlined a couple of times.

Despite that episode, I eventually began to feel better and better. Vince McMahon called and asked me to be an agent. I was 51 years old at the time, and I really did not have any hankering to be anything but a wrestler in the business, so I told him no. I had retired in 1988. We talked for an hour or so, and I kept saying no. He told me that the reason he wanted me to come on board was simple: he wanted someone who cared about the business and who would talk straight to him. Just like that, I was a member of the inner circle. But because of my health problems, I had lost my some of my spunk.

The new job definitely helped financially. I had been making about $250,000 as a wrestler, and being an agent paid about $150,000.

The job was not without migraines or a massive amount of responsibility. I hated it at first. They had me doing everything from handling the money to setting up the order of the matches to what kind of music would be played to making sure the security was set up. About the only thing I did not do was cook the hot dogs at the concession stands or sell programs in front of the arenas.

Vince knew I was not enjoying myself, so he called and said I would be the one who ran the show and that someone else would handle the finances. I could not have been happier. Running shows was what I was good at.

The attitude of the talent was changing. The professional wrestling business was becoming more and more corporate and I really did not like it. I came from an earlier, less structured time. Remember, we ate bologna sandwiches and drank beer. A lot of the current wrestlers dine on filet mignon and drink the finest liquor.

As an agent, if I had a problem with the talent, I would go to that wrestler first and try to handle it one on one. But at some point, I had to go to Vince. There were times when Vince wanted to be closer to the talent than to his agents, so as agents we were stuck in the middle, which was a mighty uncomfortable place to be. On the road, there could be only one hands-on boss, and that had to be the agent.

I spent nine years doing it. It was a tough job because there were always problems out on the road. One time I was told by the main office that a particularly prominent wrestling family was banned from the locker room. That was not an easy order to follow—especially since the family used to handle promotions in that town. They were also really good people, but I was told to keep the locker room clear, so I did as I was told.

Another time, I had a wrestler flunk a drug test. He was not just any ordinary wrestler, either. He was one of the superstars and I had to tell him he could not work that night. When I broke the news, he was very placid and admitted he had screwed up. A half hour later, this same wrestler lost it in the locker room. He just went berserk. He was going to kill Vince. He was going to kill me. He was going to take down everybody with the exception of the U.S. Marine Corps, the U.S. Army, and Spider-Man.

There was always something going on while we were on the road. Some of the wrestlers were prima donnas in spandex and eyeliner.

When I first started wrestling back in the 1960s, things were completely different. One day, Pat was getting her hair done and the beautician asked if she was going out. Pat said she was going to a wrestling show at Cobo Arena. The beautician said, "I'm sorry," as if she had embarrassed Pat. Twenty years later, Pat was getting her hair done. Once again, the beautician asked if Pat was going out that night, and Pat said she was going to Wrestlemania III at the Silverdome in Pontiac, Michigan. The beautician's reply: "Do you have any extra tickets?"

I remember once when we were taking a redeye out of Los Angeles to Atlanta. On the flight were five college kids who wanted to party with the WWF wrestlers. The wrestlers really just wanted to sleep. I was in first class, and I woke up as we were approaching Atlanta. There was a lot of noise coming from the back of the plane. These college kids were buying my guys drinks. The kids had obviously had plenty to drink themselves. As the kids were getting off the plane, I noticed that two girls had their tank top straps cut and were hanging loose. It looked like an outtake from *Animal House*. The boys with their buzzcuts resembled the Road Warriors more than fraternity brothers from Alpha Tau Omega. When I got home, I asked my son Dennis, who had just graduated from college, what he would have done if he had been one of the college kids on the flight. He said he would have had a great time partying with the guys from the WWF. We both had a good laugh.

There was not much laughter on another American Airlines flight from Dallas to Corpus Christi. The plane was not very full, but there was one fellow who already had too much to drink. As we were boarding, this drunk started making loud comments about the "phony wrestlers." I called the flight attendant and asked her to have the guy removed. She said that everything would be fine. So much for her powers of observation. As we started down the runway, he started getting louder and louder. Once we got into the air, he started calling out different wrestlers. We ignored him, but he kept cranking up the volume. One of the younger wrestlers went to the bathroom, and then on the way back to his seat, he dropped fecal matter on the drunk's back—not exactly a splash of Old Spice. A few minutes later, the drunk realized what had happened and he went wild. He ripped his shirt off and revealed a prison-blue tattoo of a cross. He screamed that he had a loaded .45 in his luggage and that he was going to kill some wrestlers. I told the flight attendant to have the captain call ahead and have the police meet our plane. When the police checked the drunk's luggage, they found the gun and he was placed under arrest.

It was not just drunks who potentially could shoot down things related to wrestling. So could Mother Nature. We had a sold-out arena in St. Louis and nearly everybody was there to see Hulk Hogan. The Hulkster had been held back at the office in Connecticut to do some television work and was traveling separately by Lear jet. Unfortunately, a heavy fog had descended and the airport was shut down. I got a call and was told that Hulk was circling, hoping to land to make the show, but he was already late.

Soon, we had to make an announcement that the fog was keeping Hulk from landing. I have always believed in being honest with the fans. They were also told that if Hulk could not make the show the event would be replaced by an exciting battle royale. They were offered a refund and had until the fourth match to get to the box office. Only about 700 asked for a refund; the rest stayed for the show. Hulk never made it. I had the weatherman on the 11:00 PM news tell the folks in St. Louis that the area fog was so bad that it beat even Hulk Hogan.

Wrestling had become part of the family entertainment mainstream. Business was growing, and a big part of that business was merchandising. The sales of bandannas and T-shirts and action figures were exploding. Rather than the independent contractors who used to populate the wrestling ring, the new breed of wrestlers were employees. Lots of them became legends in their own minds. Story lines took the place of ring psychology. Great physiques became more important than talent. Wrestling was passing me by. After nine years as an agent, I let it fade in the rearview mirror.

CHAPTER 15

Divine Intervention

Today, I have no symptoms of Crohn's, more than two decades after my diagnosis. The doctors cannot explain it. I have learned that sometimes medical science falls a little short. Sure, doctors can perform wondrous acts, but you also are left to wonder at times. Folks go in to have a bunion removed and leave with an amputation. Others check in for cosmetic surgery and come out looking like Mickey Rourke. Miracles cannot be collated, categorized, and placed in a medical textbook. Give a doctor five loaves and two fish and he'll order blackened tilapia with a bread basket and a glass of wine.

So, doctors cannot explain why my Crohn's disappeared. But I can. I knew God had plans for me—I just don't know what. Maybe he needs a bouncer to help St. Peter up in heaven. Maybe he took a look at his flock and did not see any other drooling, babbling, bald-headed professional wrestlers.

I had been raised a Baptist, and our stern preacher looked down from the pulpit and intoned that all sinners were going to hell. Now,

I liked hot weather as much as the next guy, especially when it came accompanied by a swimming pool and a baseball diamond. I had not been a really bad kid, but even by the time I was seven or eight, I figured I was already damaged goods. Swipe a piece of Dubble Bubble or two and you are earmarked for eternal damnation? Pilfer some licorice and the thermostat gets turned up for eternity? It hardly seemed fair, but I shrugged my shoulders and figured that's the way things go.

After that scare, it took me years to put the welcome mat out in front of my life again.

Even if there was a God—and back when I was younger I figured the odds of that were longer than George "the Animal" Steele winding up as top dog in a Dale Carnegie class—I did not figure I was a VIP. The only way I was going to bust through the pearly gates was with some bolt cutters, a couple of sticks on dynamite, and an 18-wheeler.

But God for some reason took enough interest in me to cure my Crohn's, and he handled the damage from plenty of other things as well.

I have walked on the edge most of my life. I was never a member of the National Honor Society. I was never in Boy Scouts, much less a troop leader. I was also never much of a reader because of my dyslexia, and that included the Bible.

On the plus side, I never broke any laws. All right, I did not break any *major* laws. I never served time in jail. But I do not want to give myself too much credit. I got in plenty of fights as a teenager. "An eye for an eye" was a credo I could relate to. "Do unto others" was another one that I could have cross-stitched onto a doily and hang on the wall. My idea of the Golden Rule was usually tinged in black and blue, with some blood dripping from the words, for good measure.

It was only later that I realized God gave us the air that could be used to pump up footballs and basketballs and athletics, thereby keeping me in school and close to the right path. My dad stuck me at that infernal desk and he did it both with his firm grip and God's own hands. That created goal-setting, something I have used in many situations over the years. I had many blessings that I did not recognize for the longest time, and I now truly believe that God had a plan for me.

Granted, it might seem like a strange blueprint. Saddle the kid with dyslexia in a world in which nobody even knew what that learning disability was. Sit him at a desk in the living room of his house where he tries in vain to learn while his friends play in plain view, in the schoolyard across the street. Allow him to exorcise his frustrations by knocking the bejabbers out of people in fights. Let him wrestle with the hieroglyphics of the three *R*s and turn him into a professional wrestler who gnaws on people and turnbuckles with equal ferocity. Don't tell me that God does not have a sense of humor.

But God gave me athletic ability and that truly was His blessing. Athletics opened the doors of opportunity to me, first at Madison High School and later at Michigan State University. He blessed me with Pat, and we were already married and the parents of Felicia when I got to East Lansing in the spring of 1956. Thanks to the immense help and support of Roy Niemeyer, my enrollment counselor, and my wife, I was able to earn my degree.

While at Michigan State, I took a class that taught the theory of evolution. That is the work of Charles Darwin. I presume you know what evolution is all about. Basically it says we crawled out of the slime. What started out as a tadpole is now Tom Cruise. What began as a slug is now Angelina Jolie. King Kong turned into King Kong Bundy. Or something like that.

That was all it took for someone like me who was still in the clutches of a guilty conscience dating back to those pieces of bubble gum. Seemingly doomed to a life of sweat, insatiable thirst, and an inadequate supply of Right Guard in Hell, I was convinced that science knew best and I turned my back on my Christian upbringing. The Bible was a storybook, nothing more than *Aesop's Fables* with a repetitive bottom line. Science was the real truth.

While teaching and coaching presented a great opportunity to reach plenty of people, I was not yet prepared to deliver the real message.

Wrestling put me in front of millions. Can you imagine the people I could have reached if I'd had the ability to deliver God's word then I could have made Billy Graham look like a country preacher. But I did not truly believe, so what would I have said? I did not understand how good God had been to me and my family. I let that chance slip through my hands.

Instead, I chased Bruno Sammartino around the ring. I battled the likes of Hulk Hogan and ogled Miss Elizabeth. I acted like I could not talk when I could have had so much to say. I lived two separate lives. Jim Myers was a teacher, coach, husband, and father; George "the Animal" Steele sometimes lived a life that defied definition.

It took 10 years of enduring a life-threatening disease to get my attention. It took the support of my wife, my family, and so many others. It took a 911 call and being pronounced dead in the hospital. It even took a hose attached to the muffler of my car to get my attention.

God had bigger plans for me. John the Baptist wore beggar's robes and ate honeycomb; I wore wrestling garb and ate the stuffing out of turnbuckles. God does not always pick those who shop at Brooks Brothers and wear spit-shined shoes. He does not always put us on pulpits. Sometimes, it is televised wrestling events or gurneys in hospitals or on the pages of books.

I received an e-mail from Todd Curcio, a wrestling fan. To this day, I cannot believe how simple it was. Todd asked me if I had accepted the Lord Jesus Christ as my savior. I said no, and Todd asked if I would mind if he sent me a couple of books. At about the same time, John Randolph, a minister in our family, sent me another book to read. I finally started to understand what I had missed when I was a kid wracked with guilt about swiping a couple of pieces of bubble gum and some licorice.

We were living in Florida when I told Pat we should go shopping for a church. We decided we would start at a Baptist church, just to eliminate the possibility, and then move on. It just so happened God was sitting two pews up and a couple of seats over that day. He was wearing an Izod shirt, shorts, and sandals. He was there to show me that the church was not the problem—the problem had been me.

We were surprised to see so many young people the day we visited the First Baptist Church in Merritt Island. That obliterated the stereotype I had formed years ago—that churches were filled with row after row of gray hair and wrinkles. As teachers, both Pat and I liked being around young people. We also really liked the minister. He was not all pomposity and Pepperidge Farm stuffing. He seemed like a good guy with a common touch. There was a young gospel singer from Australia giving her testimony that morning and a concert in the evening. She had the voice of an angel minus the harp, wings, and flight plan filed with the FAA.

Two days later, a hijacked airplane slammed into the World Trade Center in New York City. Then another one slammed into the other tower. Another scarred the Pentagon and one more slammed into the Pennsylvania countryside. If ever a nation was looking for answers that day, it was America. What kind of hate shapes a heinous act like that? What kind of God allows that sort of carnage? As a Christian, I was supposed to be filled with love, but hatred soaked me like a cold sweat. After mourning with the rest of the nation, it was back to the First Baptist Church in Merritt Island. We live in Cocoa Beach, an area commonly referred to as the Space Coast. The pews were filled, and many of the worshipers were in the military. It was a very emotional, very impactful day in my life.

We continued to attend the First Baptist Church and finally decided to join the congregation. We were baptized on Pat's birthday, June 16, 2002. A communion wafer took the place of way too many years' worth of steak, beer, and the stuffing from turnbuckles. We joined a Sunday school class, and I was quite a sight. Even though I had lost a lot of weight from my wrestling days, I still was recognizable as George "the Animal" Steele. Not exactly somebody with a halo.

But since I nearly visited death before I knocked on God's door, I certainly paid attention this time around when Pat and I were at church.

For Christ died for sins once for all, the righteous for the unrighteous, to bring you to God.

That's what Peter said in the Bible, and believe me, God's forgiveness was great news. I, like most of us, needed plenty of forgiveness. It was not just Dubble Bubble, either.

Yet to all who received Him, to those who believed in His name, He gave the right to become the children of God.

That is what John said in the Bible, and he and Jesus became quite a tag team. They were better than some of the great teams, such as Professor Tanaka and Mr. Fuji, the Samoans, and Jules and Chief Strongbow. He leaned on Jesus during the last supper the same way I've leaned on God.

... if you confess with your mouth, "Jesus is Lord," and believe in your heart that God raised Him from the dead, you will be saved.

That is in the book of Romans. It is Chapter 10, verse nine.

Here is a prayer from the website of the First Baptist Church in Merritt Island: "God, I admit that I'm a sinner. I believe You sent Jesus who died on the cross and rose from the dead to pay the penalty for my sins. I ask in Jesus' name that you forgive my sins. I place my faith in Jesus as my Savior, and I commit to live for Him the rest of my life. In Jesus' name, Amen."

I was sure that God had a plan for us, but I still was not sure what it was. When the timing is right, God will lead me in the right direction and I will be prepared.

Two months after we accepted the Lord Jesus Christ as our personal Savior, I met Carl Kerby. Carl is very involved in the creation movement and he provided me with the foundation that I needed. I now understand the Bible is the history of the world from the beginning of time.

According to the biography on Carl Kerby's Reasons for Hope website, his passion "is to proclaim the authority and accuracy of the Bible and to engage the minds and hearts of believers and unbelievers in today's culture so that they may experience the realities of the Word of God."

Whether he speaks to youth or adults, large or small crowds, churches or schools, Carl has a way of connecting with almost everybody, and that is one of the reasons he is a much sought-after speaker both in the United States and abroad. He has spoken in Bermuda, Canada, England, Greece, Israel, Jamaica, Japan, Mexico, the Philippines, and Wales, among other places.

Carl was a founding board member of Answers in Genesis for 10 years and served there for more than 15 years before stepping out in faith to become president and founder of Reasons for Hope. Though Carl has played many roles in his life—son of a professional wrestler, air-traffic controller at O'Hare International Airport—his most cherished accomplishment is his 30-plus-year marriage to his wife, Masami, and his role as a father to his daughter, Alisa, and his son, Carl Jr., and grandfather to his grandchildren, Trey, Naomi Joy, and Mari Hayashida.

My life has been lifted by simply accepting the Lord Jesus Christ. I am working on living my faith. I have a motto: "Let go; let God handle it." I am learning and I love it.

I am sure a lot of my buddies who I grew up with are rolling their eyes reading these words. Smacking people around is not exactly like attending the seminary. Same goes for a lot of people I met both in the ring and outside of it. If there were prayers being uttered during a match, they usually had something to do with not letting someone else tear a limb asunder. A lot of folks have a tendency to find God at about the same time that serious trials and tribulations have accosted them. I guess that partially tells my story, and I cannot deny it. For the longest time, I resided in darkness, even as my life was bathed in the ring lights.

Animal

They say that hindsight is 20/20 and as I got closer to finishing this book I started to get a much better understanding of my life, and maybe a truer understanding of my purpose. My walk through life made absolutely no sense whatsoever. Looking at things through a rearview mirror, I finally get it.

Obviously God has a sense of humor. He also has a plan. It has been a great ride; one that I hope continues for a long, long time. Sure there have been some potholes along the way. Some blood and scar tissue, too.

CHAPTER 16

Impactful Moments

Cops dust for fingerprints. They do it to bust the bad guys. You know, the jerks that break into cars or bars or banks and leave smudges behind. Every fingerprint is unique.

Teachers and coaches leave plenty of fingerprints, too. Although hopefully, most of those imprints are positive. Go to your 25th high school class reunion, listen in, and what are people still talking about? Sixth-period biology class? What about the English lit class they had with Mr. Ross? Nope—nine times out of 10 they are talking about sports. They are drawing football plays they used to run on cocktail napkins. They are recounting touchdown passes that seem to become more miraculous every time they tell the story. They are talking about their coaches. Sometimes the adjectives are positive; other times they are more profane. Take a look around Madison Heights. There are all sorts of fingerprints left not only by me but the entire Myers family.

The high school team used to play at Varsity Field, which is where Huffman Park is now located. The Madison Heights Wolverines, a youth football organization, use it as a practice field. That outstanding organization introduces youngsters to the ways of the gridiron. The Wolverines do it gently at first, offering flag football for the smallest kids. Pretty soon, though, things get more physical. Nobody yanks on flags; they smack into one another.

"Mr. Myers was also part of the Wolverines," said Al Morrison, president of the Madison School Board. "Every time I'd go out on the field, he was there coaching or helping out. He was not hard to spot. He stands out in a crowd."

I don't doubt that. I'm pretty easily noticed—and it is not because I've got Robert Pattinson's spiky hair or Liberace's fashion style. When you are big and bald and have a tendency to glower on occasion like I do, you are not easily mistaken for a plush toy from Disney.

Morrison was a two-way lineman for the Madison Eagles. He graduated in 1979.

"I remember the first time I ever went to a high school football practice," continued Morrison. "I was a ninth grader and I was heading out to the practice field behind the high school. Coach Myers saw me from where the varsity was practicing, and shouted, 'Hey, big boy, come over and practice with the big fellas.' I just smiled and continued to run to meet the freshman team. From that point on, he always had a smile and a remark and a pat on the back. While Coach Myers was the first one to point out your mistakes, he did it in a way so you understood why you did something the right way. It was not just on the football field or wrestling mat. It was in the hallway or the classroom, too. He was always offering instruction. Coach Myers was definitely an intimidating person, but once you got past that, he was a very warm and caring person."

Warm and *caring*. Those are not words that have been used to describe yours truly very often. *Mean* and *loathsome* have been more common frames of reference. *A* and *hole* have been linked on occasion, too.

"We were average, but if you ask the guys 30 years later, we won every game," said Morrison, laughing. "What I do remember more than anything is that it was more like a brotherhood than anything else."

I'll never forget the day Al decided to punk me—my vaunted fear factor had no effect on him, apparently. He had purchased a Tor Johnson mask from a Halloween shop. I walked into the gym to teach a class, and there was Al, wearing the mask, one of my own black sweatshirts, and one of my personal silver whistles hanging around his neck. I took one look at him, felt my face to make sure I was who I thought I was, shook my head once to confirm the fact, and then I walked out. I figured I was already in the gym teaching the class.

"I remember when I walked into the gym class, everybody looked at me in shock," said Morrison. "They thought Coach Myers was going to kill me for wearing the mask and dressing up like him. I had snuck into his office to grab his standard black sweatshirt and whistle. I was even carrying a clipboard like he carried."

It was an outstanding practical joke. In real life, fear factor was counterfeit. It was better suited for the wrestling fans than high school students. It's always great to have that Animal façade in your back pocket, but it is not something you want to overuse—at least not when you are teaching and encouraging high school students.

I always tried to make sure students got involved. Sure, that usually meant athletics, but it could have been anything. I hated to see anyone just sitting around. I'd tell kids that even if they were just on the couch at home, they should try to learn something, even if it's just how to shuffle a deck of cards with one hand. Then, at the very least, they would be engaging communication between their brains and their bodies.

Jerry Binkley graduated in 1977 from Madison High School. He played football for me, but probably not as much as he would've liked. Like me, when he was in high school, Jerry never seemed to take the easy path.

"I was a junior, when, in the fall of 1975, we went eight and one," said Binkley. "Only I got kicked off the team after about the fourth game. I got caught drinking in the school parking lot."

Drinking is a matter of interpretation, I guess. If drinking means taking a tiny sip of beer, then Binkley was guilty. If drinking is getting about the same amount of liquid that a hummingbird gets when he sticks his miniscule beak into one of those bird feeders, then Binkley was guilty. But if drinking is rearing back with a beer bong like Will Ferrell in *Old School*, then Binkley was innocent as a newborn baby.

But thrown into the court of Jim Myers, he was guilty as charged. No defense attorneys were allowed in my jurisdiction. Rules were rules and Jerry got kicked off the team for the remainder of the season.

"I was in the parking lot with two guys I shouldn't have been with. I had shop class, but I cut it and they had some beer in the car and were passing it around. They asked me if I wanted a drink and I told them no. They asked again and I said, 'All right, I'll just have a sip,'" said Binkley.

It was just about that time when the shop teacher, who was also an assistant football coach, burst out of school and into the parking lot. Jerry was caught red-handed and slightly wet-lipped.

That was the end of his junior season in football. His senior season nearly ended before it started, too. Jerry began to hang with the wrong crowd. (I'd had some experience with that, too.) There was not a pocket protector or a 4.0 grade-point average in the group. They began breaking into places. They took some things and they got caught. Jerry, at the ripe old age of 17, was thrown into the county jail. That is where he spent pretty much the entire summer between his junior and senior years of high school, or at least a 45-day chunk of it.

"I got out of jail on a Friday and football practice began that following Monday. When I showed up for football practice, Coach Myers told me he did not know if he was going to let me play or not, and he would have to think about it. I went over to Ken Dallafior and Dave DeGain very upset and told them I did not think I'd be able to play. They were the team captains, and they were good guys who came from good families," said Binkley.

I did think about it for a while. I am not a guy who passes judgment quickly. I did not exactly spend all of my youth kneeling at the pulpit, either, so I had a fair amount of compassion. But Jerry's résumé was not without its faults. He'd been busted for drinking as a junior. It was not even six months later when he was busted for B&E and sent to jail. Two years of probation were tacked on. He who lives in a glass house shall cast no stones? Forget the stones, I was worried about Jerry shattering team unity. Finally, I relented.

"Coach Myers told me that he would allow me to play my senior year, but I would play where he told me to play, not where I wanted to play. I probably should have been the starting fullback and middle linebacker, but he put me at defensive tackle and I was the backup fullback. I don't blame him; if something else had happened with me, he did not want it to be too difficult to find someone to replace me," said Binkley, chuckling.

The Madison Eagles struggled Jerry's senior year. Wracked by losses after too many players from the previous season's outstanding team graduated, Madison finished 3–6. While Jerry cannot recall if the players were the butt of any jokes in the Madison High halls that fall, there arose a certain situation where the jokes had to do with some butts.

"My sisters went to Warren Mott High School. The football team had just gotten home on the bus after a tough loss against Oxford, and Coach Myers was not happy, anyway. Well, my sister was in a car with some friends and as they went by the bus that was parked to let us off at the locker room, they mooned the bus," said Binkley.

What is it they say about the best laid plans? What the girls from nearby Warren Mott did not realize is that the road leading past the Madison locker room in the back of the school is a dead end. The only exit is also the entrance. Hence, turning around and going out the same way was their only recourse. Only with yours truly blocking the road, their escape had been thwarted.

Police were called and Jerry was summoned from the locker room. Identities were established and Jerry suddenly worried that an infraction committed by his sister could and would be used against him in the dreaded court of Myers.

While that was never the case, can you imagine the lineup at the Madison Heights Police Department? "Coach Myers, do you recognize any of these derrieres?"

"I cried after my last football game that season," said Binkley. "That is how much it meant to play as a senior. I will be forever grateful to Coach Myers for letting me back on the team."

Jerry was the junior varsity football coach at Madison High School in the fall of 2012. He is employed at a middle school in the district. He has coached youth football in the city for more than three decades and his Wolverines have enjoyed unparalleled success over those years.

"I remember after I graduated when Coach Myers came over to the Wolverines' practice field and complimented me on how well I had been doing. Then he asked me if I would come join his staff at the high school," said Binkley. "I did just that in the fall of 1984. One of the district's assistant superintendents did not like me very much, and Coach Myers said there was a chance I would not get paid. He said if that was the case, he would pay me himself."

While Jerry thoroughly enjoyed himself and did a great job for us, he could not coach at the high school the following year because of work conflicts. The fall of 1985 turned out to be my final coaching season at Madison. I started wrestling full-time in January 1986.

But Jerry has never stopped coaching. He spent 32 years with the Wolverines before returning to the high school staff in the fall of 2012.

"What do I get out of coaching? I want to coach great athletes who are also great students. I talked to my players at least every other day about their classwork. Of the thirty kids on the team, twenty-eight did very well with their grades. Two struggled, but we made sure they got help. If I can help even one bad apple improve, that makes it all worthwhile," said Binkley.

Plenty of people had written Jerry off as a bad apple, and maybe he was. But I know plenty about bad apples, because plenty of folks had me occupying that same rotten bushel for the longest time. There are always extenuating circumstances, and I knew Jerry's folks had broken up. I had dyslexia which nobody knew about. I did not read well. I did not write well. Jerry knows the feeling.

"I can understand what some of these kids are going through," said Binkley. "I do coach some kids who are coming out of Detroit and some of them do not have it that great at home. My own parents had split up. My dad had moved out and my mom probably loved me too much. She let me do whatever I wanted, and I started running with the wrong crowd. I share my story with some of the kids and I try to keep them on the right path. I got caught for B&E and the judge put his foot down. I was seventeen years old and I went to jail for forty-five days. That opened my eyes a lot."

Ken Dallafior never got pinched for breaking and entering. I probably busted him once or twice, though. Ken was one of those many young men who walked through the doors of Madison High School and encountered my sometimes intimidating presence. I was the Hulk before anyone heard of Hogan or Bruce Banner, only my face turned red, not green.

Dallafior was a rather large presence himself. He was an all-state football player, manning both the offensive end and a middle linebacker / nose guard position.

I'd put Kenny in the middle on defense, and because he was so big and strong, I did not have to play anyone at the guard positions. Rogers told Kenny to cover the entire middle, and he could. He'd have two or three people blocking him at once. He was a real stud.

All that unbridled aggression was surprisingly absent on the wrestling mat, however. Try as I did, I could never quite get Kenny to exhibit the same kind of mad-dog mentality that he had on the football field.

One night I was home talking to Pat about the wrestling team and she asked me about the Dallafior boy. It was the early part of his senior season. I told her that I was a little frustrated, because Kenny didn't seem like he was passionate about wrestling. She asked how I handled him, and I told her I worked with him every day. Pat's head snapped around when I told her I really went at him hard. I was pounding on him constantly. In my mind, I was trying to help him out. I was trying to make him tougher. In truth, he was already tough enough. He was just totally intimidated by me.

Pat asked, "Why don't you just let him have some success against you? Obviously he is intimidated by you."

The next day, that is exactly what I did. I let my arm dangle in front of Kenny's face, and urged him to take the initiative. By the time he took that arm, I was afraid I would need the jaws of life to retrieve it. I did everything I could to get away from Kenny, but he flipped me and soon had me pinned.

After that, Kenny into a monster on the mat. He went undefeated from then on and made it to the state finals. The championship match ended in a draw after regulation time expired. Kenny was even more aggressive in overtime, but no points were awarded. When they raised the other guy's hand, Kenny was livid. He started to spit a little bile. I told him to relax, that he was no longer a high school wrestler, he was a Minnesota Golden Gopher.

Truthfully, I had wanted Kenny to go to Michigan State. Darryl Rogers, who was the head coach at MSU then, came into my office one day with his defensive line coach. I was there along with Kenny and Frank Crowell, the athletic director at Madison High. Smith told Kenny to stand up and he compared his height to his defensive line coach, who was also a big guy. Rogers said, "Well, I guess he really is 6'4" or 6'5" just like he is supposed to be." To me, it felt like he was challenging my word. I did not like it and I kicked Rogers and his assistant coach out of my office right then and there.

When a coach from the University of Minnesota came to school, he told me privately that they were not that interested in recruiting Kenny. But Kenny had quality parents who raised him right; they told him to always look people straight in the eye and give them a firm handshake. I told him the same thing. Well, after being introduced to the coach from Minneosta, Kenny did all of that and the conversation soon turned to having Kenny make a visit to Minnesota. Cal Stoll, then the coach at Minnesota, had been the line coach when I was at Michigan State.

Two years later, Cal got fired and Kenny called and said he wanted to come back home and go to Central Michigan University. I told him that he was at Minnesota for an education, and a new coach would evaluate all of the players. Kenny stayed, and he became a top player at Minnesota. He became a starter and was the team captain. He became a scholastic All-American in college after being a C student at Madison.

"As a high school kid, the first thing you're impressed with is Coach Myers' size, and that alone is pretty intimidating," said Dallafior. "After you get to know him as a coach, you are still intimidated, but a trusted bond has been formed. All these years later, I am not sure the intimidation ever really left. But do you know what? Neither has the utmost respect. That has always been part of the relationship.

"You come to realize that Jim shows his love in a different way. He would be as hard on you as you can imagine. He would push you beyond where anyone else would push you. We'd do extra conditioning. There was the occasional grabbing of the face mask that precipitated face-to-face discussions at a loud volume that were maybe punctuated by a slap to the head. My older brother had played for Jim, so my parents were well aware of Coach Myers. There was nowhere to turn and absolutely no sympathy from them.

"I remember my first day of school as a ninth grader. I walked into high school and saw Jim Myers and his brother, Jack. Both were intimidating, especially for a freshman who lacked confidence anyway. Jack talked slow, with a very deep voice. My first varsity football practice came my junior year. Jim was the head coach and Jack was an assistant. I was a big kid by then and Jim had taken some interest in me through the wrestling program. He knew I had some tools and skills, but he had to pull them out of me, so he was probably a little harder on me than on some of the other players. His attitude was, I'm going to make you tougher and I'm going to make you better.

"That first practice he gave me a lesson on his exacting standards for excellence. It was called the Bermuda Drill. There were seven [tackling] dummies and I had to go blasting through each of them. It was a hot, hot day. Jim was barking at me the entire time about how that was not acceptable and how substandard my performance was. I repeated the drill and he shouted the same things at me. The third time, he joined me and dragged me through the dummies himself. We get done and I am on the ground, and Jim is over the top of me pouring Gatorade on his head. He is ready to have a heart attack. I looked up at him, disgusted and exhausted, and said simply, 'Mr. Myers, I quit.' He just returned my gaze and replied, 'Son, I know where you live and I will come drag your fat butt out of the house and your dad will tell me to give you some more.' Like I said, I knew I had no options. My only option was to get better, and the only way to get better was to understand and accept Coach Myers' high standards for excellence. That was a defining moment for me.

"That was one of his lessons that continued to serve me well in my life, whether it was football or business. Jim was right. When I got to Madison I was probably a soft kid who was way too nice, especially on the football field or the wrestling mat. It was questionable how motivated I really was. He helped me develop a more goal-focused perspective and taught me how to be more focused when striving for excellence. My parents, John and Mary, instilled that in me, as well."

Ken had a great college career and went on to play in the National Football League. He is now a very successful executive in the health care industry.

There were not many Kenny Dallafiors who came through the doors at Madison High School, but there were many kids in football and wrestling who did well. A lot of my friends come from very poor families and have gone on to be very successful, just like a lot of kids I coached. It goes back to a person's work ethic and principles. I truly believe that. Success has to be important, and determination does not have to reside in Bloomfield Hills or Grosse Pointe.

One of the reasons for our success on the wrestling team was that we became like one big family. The wrestlers, their parents, their grandparents, and the coaches all formed a tight bond.

Of course, there's not a family out there that does not have its squabbles every now and again. I remember I had a freshman who had to wrestle against our crosstown rival's best wrestler. My kid shocked everyone by going out and putting the kid on his back. My kid was ahead 8–3 going into the final period, but then the tide turned. He battled hard but got pinned. This kid, who was a little bit of a challenge to coach, threw his headgear and started to come off the mat like he was going to throw a tantrum. One of the things we always talked about as coaches was knowing how to win like champions and also how to lose like champions. I put my hands on his shoulders and start talking to him to calm him down, and the next thing I know his mother was beating me on the top of the head with her purse. We videotaped all of our matches, and when I watched the film later, there was stuff flying all over the place that had come out of her purse. Believe me, it was hilarious to see.

A few years later, Michigan Wolverines head coach Lloyd Carr came to the school to visit. We did not have anyone who could play at the University of Michigan level, but he did it just as a courtesy to me. He told me to bring some of the seniors down to the office and he would talk to them. Lloyd proceeded to ask each of them what they wanted to be. The first answered an engineer. The second kid also said he wanted to be an engineer. The third kid, the one whose mom had hit me in the head with her purse a couple of years earlier, also said he wanted to be an engineer...only he wanted to be the engineer of a train. *Choo choo!* Like I said, he could be a challenge.

Pat Coleman does not do much traveling by train. A very successful businessman, he is a first-class-flight sort of guy. A 1971 Madison High grad, he is the married father of three and is in health care administration.

"I still talk to Jim Myers all of the time," said Coleman, who today resides in Grand Rapids, Michigan. "He was originally a role model and a mentor when I was in high school and he remains a good friend and a life coach. While Jim Myers has taught me many things, the one thing he really taught me is how to deal with people. He has helped me negotiate my way through life."

Early on, I did not deliver those lessons like Socrates or Plato. The students did not gather around and look up at me placidly while I talked in platitudes. My words were probably a little less lofty, and I did not dress in robes. Pat's older brother, Paul, wrestled for me on those first two teams. Pat Coleman arrived in high school weighing 95 pounds soaking wet. He was maybe 5'5", could not run fast, could not jump high, and hated swimming, so the athletic smorgasbord set out was fairly limited for him. By default, he became a wrestler. By process of elimination, he was my wrestler.

"Jim Myers started the wrestling program in 1965 or 1966, and I got to high school in 1967. While Coach Myers was certainly very helpful, we were all learning together. We would learn new moves by looking at books. One thing he did was make sure we were in shape. If we lost, it was not because we got tired. There was not a lot known about athletic training and understanding of the body back then. Jim simply worked us into the ground. He'd run us forever and we'd be wearing those wrestling shoes," said Coleman, laughing.

All right, so there was no tai chi in the late 1960s. There was no Tae Bo, BowFlex, or even Pilates. I was not running a fitness club. Nobody was handing out warm, plush towels and sitting in saunas. This was a wrestling team. We were trying to build a program and responsible young men all at the same time. Pat was one of the best wrestlers I ever had.

"I placed in the state meet three of my four years," said Coleman. "In 1970, Berney Gonzales and I won state championships. When I was a sophomore, the team won a state championship. The next year, we were second as a team."

Pat finished with a career record of 101–8. Five or six of those losses came in his first year.

"Even when I was losing as a ninth grader, I never, ever thought about quitting. Jim Myers taught us all about determination. You just did not quit. There was no appeal process, either. If you had a problem, you fixed it, and that is one of the first things I tell all my employees to this day. If we have an issue, then we tell the client and make things right," said Coleman.

Making things right. That seems to be a novel concept these days. The dishwasher you bought six weeks ago suddenly can't clean a baked bean off a Teflon pan. The car you drove off the lot six months ago suddenly sounds like it has black lung. You go back to the appliance store. You go back to the dealer. The people who sold you the products are nowhere to be found. They, along with customer service, seem to be in the Federal Witness Protection Program.

There's no stigma attached to quitting these days, either. People used to say that when the going gets tough, the tough get going. These days, a kid will say that when the going gets tough, he's going home. Home to play video games. Home to eat way too much. Home to wallow in tortilla chips, bean dip, and self-pity.

"If it was not for Jim Myers, I would not be where I am today," said Coleman. "I would not have even gone to college. My grade-point average in high school was about 2.5, and I can remember going into my high school counselor's office and he handed me job applications to Ford and Chrysler and told me that is where I was headed because my grades were not good enough. When Jim Myers heard that, he was incensed.

"I was the only one of seven kids in the family to go to college and graduate. The number of kids from Madison High who went on to college was not that high, but of the ones who did, I would be willing to bet that Jim Myers influenced a huge number of them. First, he had a big influence on kids because he coached football, wrestling, and even track for a while. Secondly, Jim Myers never gave up on a kid. He took kids who nobody else wanted and banded us together into a team."

I knew Pat had what it took to succeed in life. Anyone who was as tough and determined as Pat was going to make good. So, I called a friend who was the wrestling coach at Grand Rapids Junior College, and that is where Pat went. After that, he earned a scholarship to wrestle at Central Michigan University.

"When I got out of college, I was a teacher and a coach in Greenville, Michigan, for a year, and Rockford for four years. After I got married, I knew I had to make a better living than what teaching offered, so I started first in the health insurance industry," said Coleman.

Health insurance very nearly was an issue when Pat, Berney Gonzales, and one of their teammates, Fred Dunning, were at the state wrestling meet as juniors. The meet that year was held in Okemos, which is close to East Lansing.

"In those days, we used to travel in drivers' training cars," said Coleman. "Jack Myers was driving and he and Jim started arguing. Jim was taking us through East Lansing and pointing different buildings out. It was his way of taking our minds off the state meet. He did not want us to get too nervous. The trouble was, Jack was famous for getting nervous. He'd get more nervous than any of the wrestlers and sometimes he would throw up. Jim and Jack started arguing. Jack started screaming, 'If you want to drive, then you go ahead and drive.' We had to be going 30 miles per hour and Jack just put the car into park. I mean, all three of us in the backseat went flying into the front seat. I was behind Jack, and I went smacking into him. Fred was in the middle, so he flew right between Jack and Jim. Berney flew into Jim. It was unbelievable," recalled Coleman, laughing again.

My brother, Jack, would like a chance to clarify Pat's story about that driving incident in East Lansing. Not that any of the particular details are incorrect, but you know how little brothers are. If they do not get their way, they will stomp their feet, hold their breath, and turn blue as a Smurf. Believe me, Jack is no Smurf. He is a tough, tough guy who got drafted by the Chicago Bears but never made it out of training camp, thanks to a cheap shot to the knee from Mike Ditka. But that is another story for another time, so let's hear Jack's side of the driving story.

"Jim wanted to show everyone where he taught at the boys' vocational school while he was at Michigan State," said Jack. "So we have to drive there and we were on Grand River Avenue, and Jim was giving me directions. We were in the left-hand lane and he wanted me to turn right. That happened at least three times, and I had just had it. I threw it into park and told him that he could drive. All right, maybe we were going a little fast to come to a screeching halt. You should have seen the looks on the kids' faces. Their eyes were as big as saucers."

Remember, these were in the days before the federal government mandated dashboards with padding that could turn a Mike Tyson haymaker into a love tap. Hitting the dash was a pretty memorable experience back then. This was also before the law mandating seat belt usage. That's why any sudden stop could be turned into an impromptu flight. Before than, using a seat belt was pretty much limited to airplanes. That is exactly what the kids became.

That was not Jack's only story about me and the vocational school in Lansing. He also tells a tale about getting in a fight there. If it has to be cross-referenced, start in the non-fiction aisle of the local library.

"When Jim was teaching at the school, I was there visiting him," said Jack. "He was walking a group back to class. I just happened to be walking nearby and Jim suddenly said to the group, 'Everybody stop!' Then he said to one of the guys, 'Ping-Pong, do you want a piece of my brother? There he is!' I had no idea what was going on. I did not hear anything Jim said. All I new was that this guy came charging at me without any warning, so I just decked him."

Wrestling was not the only sport we coached together. We were also on the same football staff. Jack graduated from Western State Colorado University in Gunnison, where he played football. He had previously spent a year at the University of Iowa, but was politely shown the door by coach Jerry Burns for getting too acclimated to college life too quickly.

Jack earned a bachelor of science degree from Western State and a master's from Central Michigan, where he also went on to earn an advanced degree in education. He started teaching physical education in high school and eventually became a superintendent.

"Jim and those guys he played sports with in high school were my heroes," said Jack. "He is seven years older than I am. I remember playing in the sand under the bleachers at the football field. I really looked up to them. Even though he's in Florida now and I am in Michigan, we talk all of the time. We are still close."

There was nothing heroic about professional wrestling, at least not as far as Jack was concerned. I took him to Pittsburgh with me and he wrestled as Professor Blood. He wore a red mask and red tights. The color scheme was ironic, because if there was one thing Jack could not stand about wrestling, it was the liberal amount of blood that flowed some nights.

"I didn't like wrestling. I did not like going through the crowds. People were always throwing stuff at me and honestly, that concerned me. I did not want to get hit by acid or something. It was just a crazy world. I would watch Bruno Sammartino after matches looking in the mirror admiring the blood on his head after he'd cut himself with a razor during the match. That was probably the defining moment in relation to me not wrestling anymore. I just thought it was stupid," said Jack.

But there was nothing stupid about the prep version in his eyes. He loved coaching the high school kids. We were together about five years. We were once at the state meet and Jack was coaching with me. It was Berney Gonzales' and Pat Coleman's junior year, and Pat got taken down out of bounds. The people began to boo and Jack asked me, "How can they be booing high school kids?" Right then, I knew we had our heat. Two ladies sitting nearby pointed at me and said, "That's the coach who is one of those pro wrestlers and he's teaching his kids those phony pro wrestling moves." I just started laughing.

"Once," said Jack, "we were wrestling Warren Mott High School and Jim Gibson was their coach. Jim Gibson was also the mayor of Hazel

Park. Two heavyweights were on the mat rolling around and the official was flashing points like crazy. I'm not sure the scorer was keeping up. After the match, Gibson heads to the scorers table to talk to the official and Jim said that he was just going to stay seated. I reminded Jim that Gibson was a politician, so Jim threw his clipboard in the air and hurried to the scorers table himself."

There was nothing political about the Madison Community Education Foundation that we formed when Jack was the superintendent. We held golf outings, dinner dances, and other events to raise money for scholarships for the kids in Madison Heights. The city is full of blue-collar folks whose budgets lean way closer to Hamburger Helper than filet mignon. They are hard-working, but getting many of the extras can be difficult.

"We felt it was necessary to give kids from our socioeconomic background a chance," said Jack. "We'd give say, thousand-dollar scholarships, where a young man or young woman could further their education at somewhere like a community college or a vocational school."

Years later, Pat Coleman found himself at a trade show in Orlando. The show was being held at a convention center and there were more than 10,000 people in attendance.

"I asked Jim if he would mind coming over and signing some autographs," said Coleman. "I just did it on a whim without any advance publicity or anything. Jim said all we needed was a laptop, and he would take care of the rest. This was three years ago, and do you know we had a three-and-a-half-hour line of people waiting for his autograph? It was unbelievable. These were grown men and they were crying when they came up to Jim and talked about how they'd seen him wrestle in this place or that place. Some had taken their kids to the matches. Others had gone with their own fathers. Jim remembered every venue and every match. It was one of the most incredible things I'd ever seen."

Most wrestling fans know me as a guy with the extremely hairy body. I looked like I had a mohair sweater on even when my torso was naked. Most high school students knew me as the guy with the black sweatshirt and clipboard. That was my fashion statement of choice in gym class and at practice. But I do know how to get dressed up. Did you know that ZZ Top wrote "Sharp Dressed Man" about me? Just ask Pat.

"Jim taught me how to dress," Coleman said. "Most kids didn't know this, but he used to come to school every day in a three-piece suit, go to his office before anyone else knew, and change into the clothes he wore for class and practice. When he was at a wrestling meet, he dressed up.

"I'm at a place in life now where I have custom-made suits. I drive my wife nuts because I have 45 pairs of shoes. When I fly, I always fly with a sport coat and sometimes a tie. Most people fly looking like they are on a bus. I am certainly not bragging, but it is all about Jim Myers teaching me how to succeed in life. Dressing well is part of it."

The wardrobe that I wore when I played the part of Tor Johnson in *Ed Wood* was a little on the understated side. Understatement was not always part of my routine.

"Here's a funny story," said Coleman. "When Jim and Pat were out in Los Angeles making the movie *Ed Wood*, I was traveling to Salt Lake City. I called and asked if they wanted to meet me in Las Vegas. Jim said, 'No way. We are in a very nice two-bedroom apartment, so why don't you come here?'

"I flew to Los Angeles and it was a Friday afternoon. It was probably a 40-minute trip back to their apartment from the airport. I asked how he got the job in the movie and Jim literally spent the entire time talking about his acting ability and how impressed Tim Burton had been with him during his audition and that sort of thing.

"When we got to the apartment, Pat opened a book and showed me a picture of the real Tor Johnson. Jim looked exactly like him and Pat said that's really how Jim had gotten the part. Jim just smiled and said, 'Oh, I was getting to that.' He truly is a showman."

I was just ribbing Pat Coleman. I love to do that sort of thing. But something I never joked about was educating kids. It probably had a lot to do with my struggles with dyslexia; I tried to never write anyone off. One person's hurdle is another's launching pad. Some folks can split the atom or sit down over dinner and discuss the theory of relativity. Others specialize in woodworking.

"Jim has always had the ability to make everyone feel special," said Coleman. "The way he looks at the world is different than the way most of us look at it. He touched so many lives as a teacher. He has that positive outlook on life, and he was able to transfer that to kids in particular. He is just so engaging."

Mike Kaufman's vocation is high school principal.

Kaufman, Madison High Class of 1971, had a rather clammy-handshake sort of introduction to wrestling when he was a high school student.

"I had played basketball my entire life. When I was a grade school player, I was the team captain. I was pretty good. But when I got into junior high, I had become a chubby little kid without any speed or height. I'd gone from a team captain to third string, and that did not sit well with me."

A three-sport kind of kid, Mike never thought about sitting on the sideline for an entire season. I was his gym teacher in the ninth grade and a section of our sweaty curriculum dealt with wrestling. Kaufman did pretty well on the mat, and I asked if he had any interest in joining the team.

"I won exactly one match as a sophomore," said Kaufman. "That was on a team that won the state championship, if you can imagine that. What kept me going? Quitting was never an option. I never, ever considered it. It just never crossed my mind. When I grew up, you never quit anything. That would've been about the worst thing you could have ever done.

"Once you got past the fact that Jim Myers was absolutely terrifying, you found out that he was a very caring individual. I wrestled at 185 pounds and he gave me a lot more slack than he did with some of the other guys who had more talent. He knew I was trying. He gave me a lot of encouragement, and that is something I'll always remember."

To me, even the kid who struggled mightily on the wrestling team was better than someone who never even bothered to try. Wrestling is a very unforgiving sport—it's just you and your opponent and that looming introspection. There is nobody to bounce-pass the blame to. There are no linemen up front blocking. Mike had the guts to get on the mat. He won more than half of his matches the next year, and as a senior he probably won three quarters of them.

"Jim Myers taught us all to never give up, to never quit, and to always persevere," said Kaufman. "I'm not sure we won many football games before our senior season, but that year when we were twelfth-graders we won the league championship. That just reinforced everything that Jim Myers taught us."

After graduating from high school, Kaufman got a job at Dodge Truck. It was originally supposed to be for no more than 89 days during the summer, because anything more than that put a guy in the union along with all the accoutrements awarded UAW members. His dad worked at the Dodge truck plant, too.

"Nobody told me to go home after those 89 days, so I just kept working there," said Kaufman, laughing. "I never worked on the line; I was an inspector. People would ask me all of the time how I got that job and I just played stupid because I really didn't know. But I was making a lot of money, and believe me, I had second thoughts about going to college and becoming a teacher. I gave up a lot of money."

But he stuck with his education. He started coaching while he was at nearby Oakland University. He kept working at the Dodge plant, and while it took him 7½ years, he graduated and became the first one from his family to earn a college diploma. He taught social studies at a middle school in Madison Heights and stayed in the district for 28 years in a variety of roles, including interim superintendent. He is now the principal at Romeo High School.

"I look at Jim Myers as a second father," said Kaufman.

Not everyone loved me at Madison High. Probably the most disturbing incident I ever had occurred during the Vietnam War era. Ron Huxtable was a young man who had been on the high school swim team, I think. I know he never played on my football teams or wrestled for me. After high school, he went off to the army and joined the Green Berets. Before he shipped out to Vietnam, he came back to school in his dress uniform. I remember seeing a crowd form outside my office. They were looking in the windows. The next thing I know, Ron burst through the door and announced he was there to kick my butt. I told him to get out of my office, but he assumed a martial arts position and lunged at me. I quickly weighed my options and I did not seem to have any, so I proceeded to grab him, lift him up, and slam him onto my desk. That pretty much ended the confrontation.

Sadly, Ron was killed shortly thereafter in Vietnam, and to this day I am not sure what precipitated that bizarre incident at Madison High. I probably had kidded him about swimming instead of wrestling, but I kidded everyone like that. I have visited the Vietnam Memorial several times, and every time when I see Ron's name I break down. The entire incident still disturbs me greatly, and I hope to see Ron in heaven someday.

Jimmy Brown is the athletic director at Madison High School now. A former all-state football player, he never played for me. He got to high school the year after I left as a teacher and a coach. That does not mean he was never on the football field with us, however. Jimmy was a water boy for our outstanding team in 1985.

"My sister and brother were both older. I was playing youth football for the Wolverines but was lucky enough to be a water boy for the Eagles," said Brown. "I actually was the water boy in 1985 and 1986. The '85 team went 8–1 and the '86 team was 9–0 during the regular season."

Those teams included players like Jimmy Burns, Rob Sparks, Kenny Smith, John Mandarino, and Dave Cavender. While they were just high school kids, they were heroic figures in the eyes of Jimmy Brown.

"Mr. Myers and those teams really drove me to love the game of football, and I guess I have bled purple and gold ever since. That is when it all kicked in for me; my love of not just Madison High but also the school district itself. If were not for the game of football, I'm not sure what I would be doing today," said Brown.

Brown, a 1993 Madison grad, went on to play at Wayne State University in Detroit. He worked in the automotive industry after graduating from college with a degree in business logistics, but returned to his alma mater in 2010.

"Jerry Binkley was my coach with the Wolverines, and he was a product of Mr. Myers. Most of the coaches I had were also products of Mr. Myers," said Brown. "Most of the success the district has experienced started with the foundation that Mr. Myers established."

Berney Gonzales was a big part of that early success. Gonzales remembers meeting me like it was yesterday. Really, it was about 45 years ago at the Dairy Twirl on Lorenz Street, which is just across from the high school. I guess I have a way of leaving an indelible mark on some folks. Sometimes that mark is black and blue.

"I was in the eighth grade, and a kid started a fight with my buddy for no reason," recalled Gonzales. "He was bigger than me, but I went with a double leg without even knowing what it was and took him down. I commenced to whipping on him pretty good and I did not know that Jim Myers was getting an ice cream at the time. Suddenly, I felt this big hand on my shoulder and turned around ready to slug the guy, but when

I looked up and kept looking up and up and up. I thought to myself, *Whoa.*

"It was Jim Myers, and he told me, 'That would be enough, young man.' Believe me, that was all it took. He was a huge, intimidating guy, especially for a kid in junior high. I did not know him personally, but my older brother, Mike, was a sophomore at the time, and Mike was on the wrestling team. Jim Myers told me I was welcome to come to the high school and get on the mats with the team. I did, and as an eighth grader I was able to hold my own."

Berney did much, much more than simply hold his own as a high school wrestler. He went on to become a two-time state champion for the Madison High Eagles. He also was a junior national champ and became the first American to win a gold medal in Greco-Roman at the Junior World Wrestling Championship in Tokyo in 1971. The year before that, he was listed on *Wrestling USA* magazine's High School All-America Team. He went on to Oklahoma State.

Gonzales has been a high school wrestling coach for about 30 years. He is now leading the program at Bishop Foley High School in Madison Heights.

"I started coaching when I was thirty-two years old and I came to realize that building champions is what I like to do," said Gonzales. "I love to teach kids how to defend themselves and how to be winners; how to understand the meaning of commitment, dedication, and drive. That is what Jim Myers taught us. They have to know what hard work means and the results it brings.

"At the end of the day, after four years, they are well-rounded, respectable young men. You can't judge their accomplishments by their won-[lost] records. Just coming in here is an accomplishment."

Berney kept coming back to the Madison High wrestling room. So did Pat Coleman, Ken Dallafior, Mike Kaufman, Al Morrison, and countless others. Not all of them were champions, but they were all winners in my eyes.

Berney might have a tough season at Bishop Foley this year. He lost nine seniors from his previous team, and there were only 10 in the room the first week of practice. Times have changed. Wrestling is a tough sport, and fewer and fewer kids seem willing to step up to the challenge. There are no cheerleaders in wrestling. There are no game programs. Sometimes, there is not even an available concession stand.

"Jim Myers told me once to not look for any Berney Gonzaleses on your team," Gonzales said. "He said you have to go with what you have, and I agree with that. Even the worst kid in the wrestling room is better than anyone in the hallway who refuses to put himself on the line.

"Another thing Jim Myers made sure we did was win like champions and lose like champions. He said if we lost, the other person was the better wrestler. It was an honor to wrestle for him. He taught us that the toughest teams mentally and physically would win most of their matches. He said you don't need a library of moves. What we lacked in skill we more than made up in guts and determination.

"Jim Myers had such a presence about him. He was a class act all the way, but when we walked into a gym, people knew it was the Madison High team. We walked in single file. It was military-like. He taught us all to be very respectful, that we would not be afraid of anyone but we would be respectful of everyone. We always knew that win or lose, he would be in our corner and he would be proud of us. That is something I have always told these kids, too."

I had no patience for kids who did not respect others. More than once I had to lead a kid back onto the mat to shake hands with his opponent and the opposing coach. That is just part of the decorum in high school wrestling. It is a far cry from pro wrestling, where you'd rather hit a guy in the head with a folding chair than show him any respect. You would use the much-vaunted foreign object on a guy before you would shake his hand. That is all part of the act, though. In the locker room after a show, we had nothing but respect for one another...at least most of the time.

217

"I remember I had a wrestler named Justin Van Tassel who taught and coached wrestling in Port St. Lucie, which was about an hour away from Jim Myers' place in Cocoa Beach," said Gonzales. "Justin would fly me, my wife—whom I lovingly calling the Warden—and Erich Swanson, my assistant coach, down to Florida to help him at his wrestling camp.

"We did that three years and we went to see Jim and his wife, Pat, every year. They were always so gracious. I remember Jim inviting all of the kids from the camp into his home, and the kids were so excited to see George 'the Animal' Steele. Jim fed them pizza and we sat around and watched some of his matches on television and he signed autographs. He could not have been more warm and welcoming, and the kids ate it up."

I tried never to forget the fans. In fact, I love the fans, even the ones who pelted me with bottles and debris over the years. All of those years when I was a heel, they were the ones who were paying me. Even the guy who came at me with a knife at the Pedro Morales match. Even when I nearly got killed trying to leave the arena in Washington, D.C., after my match with Bobo Brazil. Even that crazy mob that chased our taxi through Manhattan after my battle with Bruno Sammartino at Madison Square Garden. You have to love wrestling fans, even if they loathe you.

CHAPTER 17

Signing Off

It is a very nice sign. It is metal and it is arched and it hangs above the entrance to the football field at Madison High School. It reads JIM MYERS STADIUM.

I have always been one of those guys who equated dedications to death. A handful of years after a guy passes—that's when it is time to stick a plaque somewhere in a person's honor. Or maybe plant a tree.

So, at first I was pleasantly surprised and a little bit amused when Al Morrison called down to Florida from Madison Heights and told me they were going to dedicate the football field at Madison High in my honor. I paused, checked my pulse, and stuck a stethoscope to my chest to make sure I hadn't just met my own criteria. Al is the school board president in the Madison district. He's also a guy who played football and wrestled for me. While Al wasn't the best athlete I ever had, he certainly was not the worst. Young men like Al were the backbone of every squad I ever coached. He was a quality person and has remained one to this day.

I thanked Al and told him I was genuinely honored. Then I began to reflect on the life I have lived. What a long, strange trip it has been.

(Thanks for the lyrics, Grateful Dead. Truer words have never been warbled.)

I was thoroughly humbled and moved by the gesture, but all the while I was fully aware that it probably would not be a decision embraced by the entire community. From an early age, school was full of frustration for me. As I got more and more frustrated in class, my outlets were either athletics or fights. So, it was not surprising that some people opposed the idea when the news got out. One of the irritated parties said I had been a bully, and they were probably right. I did have my share of fights. Every punch was an exorcism of sorts, a release of the frustration I felt in the classroom when a teacher would ask me to read out loud and the words came out in hemming-and-hawing fashion.

So, I understand the objections, but that sign above the entrance to the football field means the world to me. Real impact is what your former student-athletes have taken from the huddle or the wrestling mat. Somebody buying you a drink doesn't mean anything. But somebody who used to be one of your students stopping by to say hello really does mean something.

I could be pretty tough as a teacher. I was hard-nosed even when discipline in society in general started to hit the Slip 'N Slide and authority was not respected but challenged. Suddenly, if you get a ticket, it is the cop's fault. Forget the fact that you were driving 71 miles per hour through a subdivision with a posted limit of 25. If you got benched, it was the coach's fault. Forget the fact you had skipped two practices that week and had sleepwalked through another one. If you got a bad grade, it was the teacher's fault. Forget the fact that you had not bothered to open a book since the Lincoln administration. It was everyone's fault but your own.

I always held kids accountable. If I saw a couple necking in the hallway, I would call them out on it. It was a school, not lover's lane. Believe me, I was not always a beloved guy. That was never my job. I learned that from Frank Crowell, who was a coach and athletic director when I first got hired. He told me if I wanted to be loved, don't become a teacher and a coach.

I remember when Pat and I went back to Madison Heights once for a visit. Fred Agemy was the assistant principal, and we were having a conversation when a student came up to me with a pencil and a piece of paper and he asked for my autograph. I looked at him, and he was wearing a T-shirt that should not have even been worn in a locker room, much less in the halls and classrooms. It just was not appropriate. I told him, "Son, you do not show any respect for me, for yourself, or for your school wearing that T-shirt. I'm sorry, but I will not give you an autograph." Not too long after that, the same young man came running down the hallway. He had a pencil, a piece of paper, and a different shirt on. I told him I'd be more than happy to give him an autograph.

I coached both football and track for two years at Wilkinson Junior High. The football teams were undefeated both years and we were conference champions in track my second year. I thought this coaching thing was easy. I moved to Madison High School in 1963 as a physical education teacher and assistant football and track coach. In 1966, I became both head varsity track and wrestling coach. That was also the first year that Madison had a wrestling program.

Madison had very solid football and wrestling programs. Madison won the state wrestling championship in 1969. I continued as the assistant varsity football coach until 1972. In 1973, I became the head varsity football coach. In 1981, I retired as the varsity wrestling coach. The team had some great accomplishments, including 188 wins and only 41 losses. We had won nine conference championships, five district titles, and five regional championships, along with a state championship and a second-place finish at the state meet. I was the Oakland County Coach of the Year three times, the Coach of the Year in Michigan, and the National Region Coach of the Year. Those honors are a tribute to the superior young men who I had the opportunity to work with, including my sons, who I had the chance to coach in both football and wrestling.

I continued on as head varsity football coach until the end of the 1985 season. In the 13 years that I was the head football coach, Madison won two conference championships. We compiled a 65–52 won-lost record.

It's now called the Jim Myers Stadium, but honest to the New Testament, it should be the Lois Myers Stadium. My mother truly dedicated her entire life to the young people of Madison Heights. She would put out a welcome mat where none existed before. She spent 25 years on the school board, and not a single minute of it was spent with anything else in mind but the betterment of the kids and the community.

"I just decided it was time to acknowledge the years of dedication that Mr. Myers had," Al Morrison said. "Not just his dedication as a teacher and a coach, but also to recognize the history of his whole family here. What his mother alone did in this community is amazing."

My mother might be appalled by this, but she very well might have been the one who led me to professional wrestling. It was inadvertent, of course. When she led me onto the playground to fight that day, how was she to know that someday her oldest son would be tangling with the likes of Bruno Sammartino, Pedro Morales, Randy Savage, and Hulk Hogan?

The current football field opened in either 1964 or 1965. Our kids loved it. It had a world-class rubberized track around it at the time, and we hosted the state track and field regionals nearly every year. It was a point of pride for the entire community. Frank Crowell was the athletic director and football coach. I was an assistant coach under Frank.

"Jim Myers and his family were very dedicated to the community," said Jimmy Brown, the athletic director at Madison High and a former all-state football player there. "There a lot of longtime residents on the south side of the city, and there has been a disconnect with the community and the school for a while. Dedicating the field to Jim Myers will help heal that, I think. He was the face of our program for many years. He put us on the map with the success he had. We have always wanted to keep that relationship intact."

A relationship is what saved me. A girl named Pat Randolph invited me to a Sadie Hawkins Dance on a dare. My nickname was Moose Myers and it was totally appropriate. It would've taken a tranquilizer dart or worse to calm me down while playing sports. Football back then was a legalized brawl. In basketball, I had squatter's rights on the lane. In baseball, I played first base and single-handedly besmirched Abner Doubleday's good name. But other than sports and fighting, school was worthless to me.

I was lost, and then I was found. I was found by Pat Randolph, a great student and cheerleader who was one of the shining lights in our class. Me, I was a total eclipse.

I really wanted to be liked, but my social skills were lacking. I never talked to girls. I never dated. And then that Sadie Hawkins dance changed my life forever.

It has been an incredible life. Nobody could write a screenplay of my life. I mean, what is a guy who could barely read or write doing with a master's degree? What is a high school coach who spent most of his life traveling in buses doing in limousines? What is a kid who was afraid to stand up in class for fear of being mocked doing bathed in bright lights in a wrestling ring surrounded by thousands upon thousands of people? What is a guy known for never talking doing rubbing shoulders with Oscar winners on a Hollywood movie set? What is a teenager who never, ever dated doing falling in love with the girl he would be with for the next 58 years of his life? What is the kid who figured he was headed for eternal damnation because he swiped some gum doing now embracing God's word?

I am totally humbled by the football field dedication. I just want to say thank you again to the people in my hometown. My roots are in Madison Heights and I will cherish them forever. The glory does not go to me but to the Lord Jesus Christ. Even if He never played for me.